Birdwatching At The Seaside

Living with Peregrines and Other Birds
in a
Sussex Coastal City

By

Brian Easlea

en Press

First published in Great Britain by Pen Press

All paper used in the printing of this book has been made from
wood grown in managed, sustainable forests.

ISBN13: 978-1-906206-95-6

Printed and bound in UK by Cpod, Trowbridge, Wiltshire
Pen Press is an imprint of Indepenpress Publishing Limited
25 Eastern Place
Brighton
BN2 1GJ

A catalogue record of this book is available from
the British Library

Cover design by Jacqueline Abromeit

Contents

Introduction

Brighton and Hove: the Sussex coastal city known surely more for its vibrant nightlife and other such human pleasures than for its birds and wildlife! But, as all residents know, the city is blessed with glorious countryside both well within its boundaries and extending far beyond. Thus urban lovers of wildlife and countryside fortunate enough to be living in Brighton and Hove City do not have to travel very far to be able to enjoy magnificent natural scenery and to realise what excellent wildlife habitat is within their easy reach.

It seemed Dame Fortune was certainly on my side. Not only was I living in Brighton and Hove City but in 1987 I took early retirement from the University of Sussex and so found myself with ample time to return wholeheartedly to my first love in life and a schoolboy love at that: watching birds! Moreover, I was living just five minutes' walk from two excellent birdwatching sites almost in the very heart of the city and so felt myself doubly blessed. Although one site was regarded by perhaps most inhabitants of Brighton and Hove as an unwelcome eyesore, long overdue for restoration, to the eyes of birdwatchers the derelict Brighton West Pier was an ornithological jewel without equal. The other site was St Ann's Well Gardens in Hove, a small urban park highly sought-after for its tennis courts, bowling green, children's playground, fishpond with a perpetual waterfall, flowerbeds, and an abundance of trees, many of them mature, and, profiting from the trees and shrubs, a rich birdlife providing delight to many human eyes and ears. Although at first I travelled extensively both in Sussex and throughout England with the aim of refreshing and enriching my knowledge of the country's birds, as the years went by I gravitated increasingly to these two city sites so conveniently situated for me. This little book is an account of my birdwatching adventures at these two wonderful sites.

The West Pier was, of course, quite unique. A derelict pier taken over by some scores of thousands of starlings, visiting sparrowhawks and kestrels, and then by resident peregrine falcons was a birdwatcher's dream and my observations record many of the significant avian happenings on and around this derelict jewel during the last decade of its meaningful life. Of course, the stars of the show were the fabulous and charismatic peregrine falcons which had claimed the West Pier as their own. Would that the pier's fiery demise in 2003 had never happened but now, unfortunately, my observations necessarily become a farewell testament to a unique bird sanctuary which has vanished for ever.

St Ann's Well Gardens is almost the opposite of unique

in that its birdlife without obvious star performers is no doubt in many ways similar to the birdlife of any southern English urban park which has a sufficient mixture of trees, bushes, undergrowth and grassy areas together with an enticing pond. However, it has one very special feature in its location just half a mile or so from the sea which thereby makes it a magnet for spring and autumn migrants seeking a temporary, convenient stopover. Thus each spring and autumn I find myself anxiously waiting to welcome an influx of transient visitors either just arriving from or very soon to embark on their heroic, almost unbelievable transcontinental journeys. Otherwise, my observations in this little urban park record fascinating avian happenings that might have been observed in any such southern park and amply demonstrate, I trust, the great degree of pleasure an hour's daily watching of its birdlife almost certainly provides.

Though I have not written up my observations with particular readers in mind, I do hope that all lovers of birds, whether Brighton and Hove residents or those from far afield, and no matter what their degree of expertise, will find this little book enjoyable and that it will stimulate people who do not already do so to take, if possible, a very leisurely stroll each day through their local park or green space, equipped, of course, with binoculars. Would that they could also visit their local derelict pier on the south coast but not even I can now do that! I do assume that readers can either recognise all or nearly all the birds referred to in this book or possess an adequate field guide to British birds to which they can readily refer.

During nearly all the years I noted my birdwatching observations in diary form, I did not do so with the intention of publication and at no time did I possess a camera. I realise now how valuable some relevant photos would have been and so am immensely grateful to the kind people who have provided me with CDs of their own photos to include in this book. They are Chris How, Sheila Levenson, Graham Roberts and Mr and Mrs Patrick Walkington. Bob Smith kindly gave me permission to reproduce his two excellent photos of the pre-2003 West Pier.

Not only not having a camera but also not having a computer (amazing, I know!), I relied on the kindness and superb skill of Robert Sosner in printing for me colour reproductions of the photos on the CDs and in putting those photos I wished to use in the book onto one CD for the publishers. His always willing help provided me with the last incentive I needed to take my typescript and photos to the publishers! I decided to 'self-publish' because, in doing so, I knew I would not only be able to help in the production but would own the finished product.

I would like to thank all those birdwatchers who often or sometimes kept watch with me during very cold and blustery winter afternoons at the West Pier, particularly John Reaney, together with Chris Perry and Chris Phillips, but also many others. My thanks also go to those many lovers of birds in St Ann's Well Gardens who were and still are always anxious to report their observations to the 'birdman' of the park, including a lady who one winter's day almost certainly saw a bluethroat, "a robin with a bright blue breast hopping about under a bush," but who reported her sighting to me only two weeks later! Importantly for me, it has always been a pleasure to talk to and correspond with Peter Whitcomb about his detailed knowledge of birdlife and local birds. Several other people have also been very helpful with information. In particular, I have profited from correspondence with David Warden about various aspects of bird behaviour, Roger Cooper kindly told me about his observations of birdlife at the West Pier seafront and in adjacent squares, and I am much indebted to Dr David Harper of Sussex University for a long conversation about the always fascinating behaviour of birds. Some very valiant people have kindly read and commented on drafts of parts of this book and I'm particularly grateful to, in order of their comments, Graham Roberts, Peter Whitcomb, John Reaney, Michael Crane, Laurie Keen, Chris Perry, Sheila Levenson and David Parkin. Of course, I alone am responsible for the final text.

Finally, although Brighton and Hove were awarded unitary city status only in the year 2000, I refer for convenience throughout this little book to Brighton and Hove City. And what a city! As a boy I was greatly privileged to live in a small Norfolk village graced each summer by the arrival of four pairs of marvellous red-backed shrikes; alas, the last would-be breeding shrike I saw in Norfolk was on 5th June 1989. But, happily, the wonderful city of Brighton and Hove, so rich in birdlife, has given me in compensation the privilege of watching its charismatic peregrine falcons and the many other irresistible birds which grace this effervescent Sussex coastal city!

Photo copyrights

Cover and plate 10: Mr and Mrs Patrick Walkington, a juvenile peregrine on their Sussex Heights flat balcony.

Plates 1 and 2: Bob Smith, the Brighton West Pier, pre-2003. These two photos graced the front and back covers of the 1998 West Pier Trust publication, *Walking on Water: The West Pier Story* by Fred Gray.

Plates 3 and 4: Chris How, starlings over the burnt-out West Pier, post-2003.

Plate 5: Courtesy of *The Argus*, photo taken by Jim Holden.

Plates 6 to 9: Graham Roberts, Sussex Heights and the nestbox peregrines.

Plates 11 and 12: Sheila Levenson, St Ann's Well Gardens.

Plates 13 to 19: Chris How, birds of St Ann's Well Gardens.

It is important to appreciate that the West Pier seafront looked very different in 1993–4 from its present post-2003 appearance. Where the Alfresco restaurant now stands, a derelict Milkmaid Pavilion provided shelter from the biting winds, and to its immediate east a children's boating pool, drained in winter to leave shallow pools of water, provided shelter and sustenance to visiting grey wagtails. To the west of the Milkmaid Pavilion a series of bird-friendly lawns, rockeries and bushes ended in a magnificent bush beloved by a large colony of house sparrows scavenging on scraps from kindly or unwary diners at the open-air Meeting Place Café. The Bedford Hotel which figures so prominently in Chapter 1 is, at the time of writing, known as the Holiday Inn. And, of course, in 1993–4 the West Pier proudly bestrode the often fearsome waves in all its isolated, derelict glory.

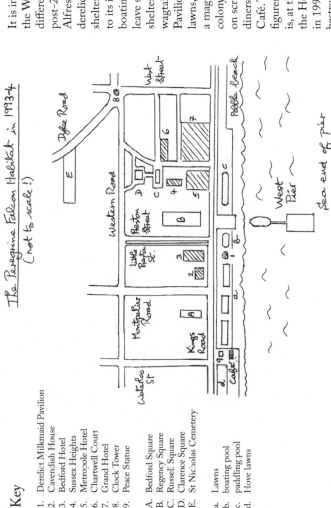

The Peregrine Falcon Habitat in 1993–4
(not to scale!)

Key

1. Derelict Milkmaid Pavilion
2. Cavendish House
3. Bedford Hotel
4. Sussex Heights
5. Metropole Hotel
6. Chartwell Court
7. Grand Hotel
8. Clock Tower
9. Peace Statue

A. Bedford Square
B. Regency Square
C. Russell Square
D. Clarence Square
E. St Nicholas Cemetery

a. Lawns
b. boating pool
c. paddling pool
d. Hove lawns

x

Chapter One

Peregrines Take to the Brighton West Pier

What an eyesore! Just how had the famous Brighton West Pier, renowned for its style and artistic elegance for over a century, been transformed by the 1980s and 90s into a decaying, derelict eyesore?

It had proudly opened in 1866 as a simple pier used only for promenading but by 1916 a large pavilion had been built in the pier head for use as a theatre and an architecturally attractive concert hall had been built between the pier head and the beach. The West Pier had basically reached its final impressive, imposing form. A quarter of a century later the Second World War grotesquely intervened and in 1940, given the threat of invasion and possible use of the pier by invading forces, the military took it over so that public use was no longer possible.

Indeed, not until 1948 was the whole pier once again open to the public but now with the theatre's two floors converted into a restaurant and fun fare and the concert hall turned into an income-earning tea room. Unfortunately, despite these changes, the popularity of the pier declined during the swinging sixties with the sad result that in 1970 the pier head was closed to the public as unsafe and the rest of the pier five years later. The Grand Old Lady had been retired. Although the West Pier Trust, created in 1978, was confident it could restore the pier and return it to profitable public use, this would obviously take much time and, to say the least, much expenditure. In the meantime, inclement weather began to ravage the pier and the Great Storm of October 1987 completely severed the link between the beach and the concert hall-cum-tea room. By this time the West Pier had become well and truly derelict and had turned into an eyesore, accusing all and sundry of its so sad neglect.

But does not every cloud have a silver lining? For birdwatchers in particular the lining of the dark cloud that was the hapless, derelict West Pier had begun to shine so brightly that it was difficult to see any cloud at all!

The Winter Daily Starling Feast

How could a birdwatcher not love the derelict West Pier? One reason, and not the least, was because scores of thousands of starlings so brutally deprived of their Old Steine tree roosting sites by that Great Storm of 1987 had decided that the West Pier was an alternative venue offering safe and secure night-time accommodation. What a joy it was to visit the pier each winter afternoon. How right I was to write in my diary on 3rd February 1992 that the West Pier was "one of the wonders of the world". No need to journey to Egypt to see *inanimate* wonders. Just a mere five minute walk about one hour before sunset each winter's day was all I needed to do to witness one of the great *living* wonders of the world.

This living wonder would build up gradually. At about one hour before sunset each day, with my gaze directed westward, I would see the first small group of starlings appear in the distance flying high over the surface of the sea straight towards the West Pier. On reaching it they would not immediately descend to its surface but on the contrary fly hither and thither hundreds of feet above it. Within a few minutes more groups of starlings would join them and eventually breathtakingly long files of starlings, comprising perhaps tens of thousands of tiny black specks, would become steadily larger until all those starlings had also arrived to join their kith and kin. After half an hour or so a huge conglomeration of flying black shapes would be twisting and turning in fantastic, stupendous, aerial gyrations until, as the sun was setting, the last of these magnificent starlings would be arriving at the pier, now skimming so low over the sea that they sometimes seemed to be only a few inches above the waves. With numbers complete, the final exhilarating manoeuvres would take place and then, in just a few minutes, all starlings would drop to the pier's surface and it would be as if nothing had ever happened - just stillness. Except on those special nights when the sea itself was sleeping and then one could hear the continual, incessant chatter of the wide-awake starlings. Did they ever sleep? Was there really so much to discuss?

Needless to say, I was not the only admirer of these starlings but because I was one of never more than a handful of watchers with binoculars quite a few of those countless passers-by who invariably stopped to gaze in wonder and bewilderment at the starling spectacle would approach me to ask three questions. What birds were they? How many were there? And why do they do it? The first question was not too difficult to answer, the second was very difficult, and the third was impossible!

No, they were not swallows or swifts! It was rather disconcerting to be asked by so many people if they were. True, there existed the ancient belief that swallows hibernated throughout the winter at the bottom of reed beds but at least it was recognised that swallows made themselves very scarce during the winter months. But directly in front of me were people in the last decade of the 20th century asking if swallows or swifts spent each long winter night, but not each short winter day, on the deck of the derelict West Pier! No, they were starlings I would explain, some of them local ones, others probably winter visitors from Scandinavia and northern Russia who had flown to far less harsh Sussex to spend the short winter days feeding and the long winter nights sleeping or chattering on the deck of the West Pier. Lots of discussion would follow about swallows, swifts and starlings and the marvels and mysteries of migration.

How many starlings were there? Only the youngest of the watchers knew for sure. A little girl of about three was adamant there were two, precisely two, while a somewhat older boy told me there were 100. To my response that I

4

thought there were more than that, he revised the number to 101. At the other end of the scale, a regular adult male watcher insisted on at least half a million. I must confess I had virtually no idea, guessing wildly at a number often well beyond 50,000 to several 100,000 or more! When I was in a playful mood I would, when asked, make up an exact and enormous number. This was usually met with a look of amazement, then a smile. Only once did I get an instant response. After my knowledgeable reply that afternoon of 114, 739, my limitations as a counter were immediately exposed. "That's funny," said the expert, "that's two more than I made it."

Why do the starlings do it? This is the really interesting question and comes in two parts. Why do the starlings, group by group, joining up at various staging posts, fly to the West Pier from wherever they have been feeding during the day, even as far as perhaps 30 miles or so away, thus expending a very significant percent of their hard-won daily energy intake? Why doesn't each group of starlings just go to roost in a convenient tree or bush near to the group's feeding grounds? And, then, even more bewilderingly, when the first groups of starlings eventually arrive and congregate together at their roost site, why do the starlings fly round and about in their magnificent swirling 'clouds' for up to one hour until the last of their number have arrived, thus expending even more of that valuable, life-sustaining energy? Such overall behaviour must have a survival advantage for each individual starling or must have had at one time but it is mighty hard to see just what that advantage is or what it might once have been.

Because so many people have asked me the question, a little discussion is certainly warranted. There is, of course, a standard answer as to why starlings roost together in such huge numbers. It goes under the abbreviation of 'safety in numbers'. For in a roost of, say, 100,000 starlings, the chance of any one starling becoming an evening meal for a hungry and determined visiting sparrowhawk is 1 in 100,000, which is clearly a very small chance indeed. And even if an insatiable sparrowhawk dines at the roost every sunset over the course of 100 winter evenings, the chance of any one unfortunate starling becoming a meal during the entire winter is still only 1 in 1000.

This, so the argument proceeds, is a much smaller chance than if the starlings roost in, say, 1000 separate sites with each site comprising 100 starlings. For at any one roost the chance in any one evening of a starling becoming a meal for a visiting sparrowhawk is 1 in 100 and if the luckless roost is visited every evening the chance of each starling becoming a meal during the winter of 100 evenings is 100 in 100, i.e. a certainty! Indeed, the initial roost of 100 will have been entirely wiped out by the end of the winter. Better by far, therefore, to be a member of a roost of 100, 000 than of a roost of 100!

But what about the remaining 999 roosting sites of 100 starlings each? If they haven't been visited by sparrow-hawks, then by the end of the winter only 100 starlings out of 100,000 will have become sparrowhawk meals, i.e. 1 in 1,000, exactly the same probability as at the one enormous roost. Certainly we can assume that more than one small roost will be visited by a sparrowhawk each evening but it seems highly unlikely that 1000 sparrowhawks will each evening find and visit 1000 small roosts spread far and wide over the countryside? And, of course, more than one sparrowhawk may well visit the huge roost each evening and there is nothing to stop different sparrowhawks from intercepting groups of starlings on their way to the one enormous roost, especially since the starlings gradually build up numbers at their various staging posts. In summary the argument about 'safety in numbers' seems gravely suspect.

Moreover, if safety in numbers were indeed the biological survival reason for starlings to congregate in such huge numbers every evening at their chosen roost site, then it would make sense to 'disappear' immediately on arrival into the safety of, in our case, the West Pier, certainly to do nothing to attract the attention of nearby raptors. But the starlings do, of course, precisely the opposite: they seemingly do everything possible to attract the attention of raptors, the twisting, turning, swirling clouds they form being visible for miles around. And raptors have very good eyesight! And raptors certainly were attracted to those scores of thousands of potential dinners seemingly inviting hungry diners to fly in and consume their fill! Those crazy starlings should fly to the pier and 'go to ground' immediately. Instead they waste valuable, life-sustaining energy by flying about for up to one hour or more, thereby inviting all starling-partial raptors to come and join them. Why?

And there were raptors that simply could not resist the invitation! On some afternoons as many as four or five sparrowhawks and kestrels would turn up to have a snack. But turning up to have a snack was one thing, securing the snack quite another! It was easy to know when a raptor had been sighted by the swirling cloud of starlings. For not only would the swirling suddenly become frenetic and agitated but often a 'suicide squad' of several hundred starlings would detach from the cloud and proceed to meet the invader, in many cases a sparrowhawk. Usually a standoff would occur for a few minutes, the sparrowhawk and the detachment of starlings confronting each other high over the pier some 20 to 30 yards apart. Eventually the starlings would charge the sparrowhawk only to see the sparrowhawk retreat but not abandon the confrontation. Only once did I see a sparrowhawk put completely to flight. Then, after two or three tactical retreats, the sparrowhawk would seemingly summon up sufficient courage (or would it just lose interest in the game?) and descend in a smooth, majestic trajectory into the main body of the pier.

Did it ever catch anything on entry? A starling? A pigeon? In the crucial last second of the dive, it was virtually impossible to follow the movement of the descending sparrowhawk. But starlings certainly were caught. Sometimes a sparrowhawk would be seen leaving the pier carrying its starling dinner; sometime the invader would be seen enjoying a starling meal on the pier's deck. And occasionally a sparrowhawk would dive straight into the swirling mass of starlings never to be seen again! Do starlings fly about in their swirling mass simply because descending to the deck of the pier before sunset would make them, as it were, sitting ducks, just too easy for the sparrowhawk to

8

grab? But once the sun has set, does darkness help them to become more elusive within the pier? If so, starlings ought to arrive as late as possible and not up to one hour before sunset and then waste all that valuable, life-sustaining energy flying about and attracting raptors! The roost behaviour of starlings is a huge unsolved ornithological mystery!

Do starlings ever forgo their aerial winter manoeuvres as the few remaining starlings always do in the summer evenings? Only once did I ever see the starlings forgo the pleasure of their sky dance to the music of the wind.

On a foul January afternoon of gales and driving rain, I somehow or other struggled to the pier to see whether the starlings would manage to arrive or not. Arrive they did, battered by the wind, drenched by the rain, but triumphant. They arrive, I thought to myself, come hell or high water. But, interestingly, as soon as they arrived, they went straight into the pier. And I saw no raptor arrive or leave that afternoon.

Magnificent and mysterious as were the starlings, they alone would not have brought me to the West Pier on so many afternoons and early evenings during the decade of years 1993 to 2003. Nor would the frequent marauding presence of sparrowhawks and kestrels have so tempted me. But the unexpected appearance of one very special raptor at the pier, one of the most legendary raptors in the entire world, proved an irresistible temptation not only to me but, of course, to many other birdwatchers. The ill-fated peregrine falcon had come to Brighton!

The December Peregrine Feast of 1993

Sussex had once been graced with perhaps more than its fair share of these magnificent raptors, its chalk cliffs holding up to about ten breeding pairs. But a dramatic national decline had begun in the 1950s with the result that by the end of the decade these iconic hunters no longer bred on the county's chalk cliffs or anywhere else in Sussex. As is now well-known, ingestion of organo-chlorine pesticides present in the bodies of their prey had resulted in peregrines being unable to reproduce. While voluntary bans on the use of DDT and other such pesticides then quickly led to a spectacular national resurgence of these flagship birds, this singularly failed to happen in Sussex. Indeed, the county had to wait until the mid-1980s for peregrine numbers to begin to increase and until 1990 for birders to be able to hear the wonderful news that a pair of peregrines had bred successfully at Beachy Head. After more than 30 barren years, the peregrine revival in Sussex had begun! By the end of 1993 it appeared that three pairs of peregrines, or more, were occupying territories in their former county stronghold.

But not, of course, in Brighton and Hove City. After all, peregrines were quintessentially wild birds of wild, wild places. And yet, in Brighton, had there not been created in the 1980s one extremely wild place, a place so wild that no humans could set foot there, a place totally exposed to the devastating forces of the merciless elements? Moreover, a place inhabited throughout the year by an abundance of irresistibly tasty feral pigeons! A place tailor-made, it seemed, for peregrine falcons. One could but dream. And then, and then….

On the morning of 9th December 1993 a leading Sussex birder, Peter Brown, kindly phoned me to say that a peregrine falcon had been seen the previous afternoon hunting pigeons at the West Pier. I could scarcely believe my ears. Presumably its visit was just a passing one-off but nevertheless…. I arrived that same afternoon, hoping against hope, and to my almost uncontrollable delight I saw a peregrine descending at great speed towards the pier from west to east and then continuing at great speed around the sea end of the pier with the obvious aim of surprising a pigeon or starling. More likely a pigeon, I thought, since the peregrine seemed large and was therefore almost certainly a female. Two pigeons made very narrow escapes, one by only a few inches. The apparent indifference of the swirling starlings amazed me. Weren't they at all concerned at the ominous presence of this fearsome predator circling their sleeping quarters? Apparently not. Well after sunset when it was almost dark and the starlings had already entered the pier, the peregrine likewise entered the pier to roost – or so I thought.

The following afternoon I arrived in good time to see the peregrine catch a pigeon without even trying by just colliding with it, and half an hour later I watched it leave the pier to perch, to my very great surprise, on one of the balconies of the Bedford Hotel from where it gazed down at the traffic some 70 feet below. There had now been three consecutive days of peregrine presence. Were the inhabitants of Brighton and Hove to be privileged

11

with the daily presence of a peregrine at the West Pier? I certainly hoped so.

I could scarcely wait for the fourth consecutive afternoon and arrived at the pier more or less still munching my lunch. Patience! After about half an hour I saw a sparrowhawk leave the pier and soar to a great height before disappearing to the east. Another half hour passed then I suddenly noticed the now familiar shape of a peregrine gliding over and about the sea end of the pier. A few more exciting minutes passed by and a kestrel came into view, flew for a time near to the peregrine and then far above it before gliding high in the sky and bombing down spectacularly into the pier. During this time the peregrine had been flying continually around the pier but had singularly failed to catch a pigeon and after a few minutes it followed the kestrel into the pier to roost for the night – or so I thought. However, I continued to watch the pier carefully, knowing the peregrine had flown to the Bedford Hotel the afternoon before. I saw nothing. Eventually, feeling much like a block of ice, I decided to head for home but with a check on the balconies of the Bedford on my way. And there, five balconies from the top in exactly the same spot as the afternoon before, perched the peregrine. As I looked in astonishment at it, I'm sure I saw it wink at me! I was cross with myself: for goodness sake, be more alert!

The following afternoon was wet and windy but after arriving at the pier I had only a 15-minute wait before the peregrine appeared and, to my great satisfaction, set about dive-bombing around the pier from high over the tall seafront building of Cavendish House. Eventually the falcon disappeared into the pier to emerge triumphant a few minutes later carrying a starling, much to the consternation of the scores of living ones. As if to rub salt into their vicarious wounds, the falcon circled the pier several times with its trophy before I lost sight of it. Soaking wet I left the front around dusk but as I passed by the Bedford Hotel I looked up and there was the peregrine on its perch. This time, though, I was given no wink that I could detect!

On my next visit, three days before Christmas, I watched somewhat incredulously as the peregrine hunted continually for 45 minutes with no success at all. Profiting from a strong south-westerly wind, the falcon would float in the updraft to high over the Bedford Hotel and then bomb down around the sea end of the pier at tremendous speed, returning to the hotel if the dive was unsuccessful. And unsuccessful it always was. Although these peregrines are certainly great fliers, I thought to myself, someone ought to show them how to catch pigeons! The following afternoon I could only repeat this comradely recommendation when during 20 minutes I watched the presumably frustrated peregrine make 13 unsuccessful dives at pigeons and starlings. Perhaps it hunted successfully in the mornings, I thought, which meant that in the afternoons it was just practising dives or even just diving for fun. So on Christmas Eve I went to the pier at noon but there was no peregrine to watch. However, when I returned in the afternoon there was my not-so-fearsome friend (as I now wished to regard the peregrine) installed on its favourite Bedford Hotel perch. Eventually it began to hunt, this time patrolling the sea end of the pier for one whole hour but without any success at all. There were pigeons galore and innumerable starlings but this most feared of raptors hadn't managed to come close to catching anything. In a bitterly cold wind I racked my brains as to what could be wrong with this peregrine!

Christmas Day afternoon was very pleasant because I was joined at the pier by two friends, the very experienced Sussex birder Peter Whitcomb and his wife Margaret. Impatient as we were to see action, we had to wait for at least an hour before the peregrine, all this while visibly dozing on the pier, decided to do some flying. In just five minutes of wing-stretching it made what seemed like one, solitary, half-hearted attempt at catching a starling and then returned to perch in the pier. It was all very strange. The West Pier was a supermarket of readily available pigeons and starlings but not one of them had seemed destined to provide the peregrine with a Christmas meal. Moreover, I had been watching this falcon hunting on eight separate occasions and had only once seen it catch a pigeon – by accident! And just once it had emerged from the pier carrying a starling. Had this also been the result of a fortuitous encounter? Or was the starling already dead? I was beginning to have very serious doubts about the fearsome reputation of peregrine falcons.

Interestingly, when next I saw the peregrine it did no flying but suddenly it produced a pigeon from somewhere, perhaps from a nearby cache of food. But given its lamentable catching skills, how had it managed to compile a cache of food in the first place? On the following afternoon it did a few minutes of flying but it was from a perch in the pier that it took a dead pigeon, in fact from an adjacent gutter a fellow watcher told me. I was appalled; this peregrine was a carrion eater! At least a visiting kestrel put on a brief flying display and, as usual, the starlings were magnificent.

The very next day something truly remarkable happened and it was not that the peregrine actually managed to catch a pigeon! On arriving at the pier I immediately saw the peregrine floating high over the Bedford Hotel from where it descended at great speed before ascending, just as it reached the sea end of the pier, to fly straight into an approaching pigeon. The hapless pigeon dropped like a stone towards the sea but the peregrine caught it in mid-air and amidst flying feathers took the partially denuded pigeon into the pier, presumably to eat it. Twenty minutes later the peregrine emerged and to my astonishment, while flying back to the Bedford Hotel, it was mobbed by a pigeon! In over seven years of fairly intensive watching of peregrines this was the one and only time I have ever seen a peregrine falcon attacked by a pigeon! It was an attack disdainfully ignored by the falcon and the rather foolhardy pigeon was left to fly off unscathed. Seemingly in a good mood the peregrine ascended high over the Bedford Hotel and then, descending very fast, flew straight towards a herring gull which took rapid evasive action. Surely, I thought, the peregrine was just playing. Whatever the case, it then flew to its balcony roost on the Bedford Hotel where it was still dozing when I left late in the afternoon. And what an afternoon. I had actually seen the peregrine both take a pigeon and be mobbed by a pigeon! I could scarcely wait for the next year's peregrine watching to begin.

But it wouldn't be a year's watching of peregrines in general but of one particular peregrine and already, to me, a very special and unique peregrine. I decided to give this falcon a name. Since it – or, rather, she – seemed to spend so much time dozing on her favourite Bedford Hotel balcony – of course, not really dozing at all but very alert indeed – I decided, in jest, to call her Dozy. Certainly it seemed to me that for as long as the West Pier remained in its wonderful derelict state not only would the magnificent starlings always use it as a winter roost, accompanied by hundreds of feral pigeons, but the peregrine I'd now christened Dozy would continue to patrol it and perhaps in time be joined by a male peregrine to form a breeding pair. It was fascinating indeed to see just what did happen between 1st January 1994 and the critical day of 23rd March 1998.

The Fantastic Peregrine Year of 1994

Throughout January Dozy provided excellent watching. On the very first day of the year, after two unsuccessful pursuits from her Bedford Hotel balcony, she flew very fast downwards as a party of some ten pigeons approached the pier from the west, came up from both behind and underneath them and seized one before any of them were aware of impending danger. Once a pigeon knows a peregrine is pursuing it, then, it seems to me, the pigeon is very likely to escape. Peregrines do best in stealth attacks, as on this occasion. After her obviously succulent dinner on the pier was over, Dozy returned to her Bedford Hotel balcony from where she was still keeping watch on the world when I returned homewards.

The following afternoon I failed to see Dozy but in compensation, just one afternoon later, I saw her catch an unaware pigeon with a fast straight approach. Two pigeons caught in two sightings in three visits! She is improving her hunting technique, I thought. In December I had seen her catch only two pigeons in 11 sightings in 11 visits. Two successes in two sightings is a lot better than two in eleven! Would this improvement be maintained?

It wasn't, at least as far as I could see. For on my next five sightings Dozy simply failed to catch a pigeon, despite apparently trying hard and indeed on two occasions she delighted watchers with superb flying displays, in one of them diving continually from and returning to high over the Bedford Hotel approximately every two minutes. Immediately seduced by Dozy was the Sussex wildlife artist, John Reaney, in whose company from then on I would often enjoy watching that fearsome but seemingly quite incompetent, would-be catcher of pigeons. Would Dopy, I wondered, have been a more appropriate name? But just two days after having this insulting and totally unworthy thought, I saw Dozy actually hit a pigeon in a full-blooded dive, though only to see her rather fortunate quarry bounce off her and fly rapidly away. Undaunted, Dozy kept trying and eventually she did manage to catch a pigeon which I saw her plucking on the deck of the pier. A third success, therefore, in a total of eight sightings. Not too bad, I thought. Moreover, on my very next sighting of her Dozy caught another pigeon after a determined flight and then disappeared into the pier to consume her supper. The following day I went to the pier both in the morning and afternoon, each time seeing Dozy diving and hunting but unsuccessfully. It occurred to me once again that Dozy did not always hunt seriously but often was just diving and hunting 'for fun'. On the afternoon of 26th January I and four other watchers all had a good laugh when after an hour's hunting Dozy caught a pigeon and then took it to a bench in the pier's Maynard's Kiosk where she plucked and ate it. We all knew that Dozy was a very special peregrine even if her table manners were not exactly, let us say, impeccable. In my final two visits to the pier in January a kestrel unsuccessfully hunted starlings, a sparrowhawk left the pier empty-handed and Dozy put in an appearance on both occasions, the first time probably catching a pigeon beyond the sea end of the pier after a truly thrilling chase and the second time doing a bit of nonchalant flying, then apparently taking a pigeon from her larder and disappearing with it. All in all I had made 15 visits to the pier through January, had seen Dozy hunting on 12 occasions and had seen her catch five pigeons.

February proved an exciting month with once again Dozy being the star performer. It was dry, sunny and windy on my first visit and Dozy simply revelled in the propitious conditions. She turned up late in the afternoon and put on a spectacular display, flying to the Metropole Hotel as if to hit it, then rising almost vertically in the updraft before diving down at tremendous speed around the pier. Woe betide any pigeon she hits, I thought. Dozy hit two. The first one simply bounced and flew away very fast. The second was likewise hit at top speed but this time Dozy managed to cling briefly on to the pigeon before it somehow or other fluttered free to disappear beyond the front of the pier with Dozy in hot pursuit. To my total amazement and disbelief Dozy reappeared from behind the pier without the pigeon. It was clearly not going to be her afternoon. A little later, from high over the Bedford Hotel, Dozy crashed down at tremendous speed towards a party of a dozen or so pigeons flying over the sea towards the pier but badly mistimed her dive and made no contact. Definitely not her afternoon. After half an hour of this thrilling endeavour Dozy herself seemed to reach this conclusion and retired to the superior Metropole Hotel to spend the night. Was the Bedford no longer good enough for her?

No Dozy on my next visit but the following day she appeared in mid-afternoon and after 15 minutes of spectacular flying she simply collided with and held on to a pigeon while gliding round the end of the pier. Sometimes it's possible to try just too hard, I thought. This wasn't the first time Dozy had caught her supper in this seemingly effortless way.

Presumably Dozy was feeling well fed for on the following afternoon she just loafed around. How different two days later when watchers were treated to another instalment of Dozy's thrilling and spectacular flying but all to no avail. Finally, she dived at high speed from behind and under an incoming party of some 20 pigeons and came up through the middle of them when it seemed much, much easier to have collided with one. Dozy then retired to the pier and after a few minutes took something from her larder. There was to be no more hunting.

The afternoon of my next visit was calm and sunny, not good Dozy conditions and, sure enough, when I arrived in mid-afternoon I could see no Dozy. After an hour's waiting there was at least some action when a sparrowhawk bombed down spectacularly into the mass of starlings and disappeared behind the sea end of the pier. This was followed by two kestrels displaying together high above the various hotels before one of them, as had the sparrowhawk, bombed down into the cloud of starlings and disappeared from view exactly as had the hawk. Three swans flew past the sun as it set over the sea – absolutely beautiful. In contrast to the cormorants assembled at the end of the pier, the three shags below them looked appealingly diminutive, one sporting a very nice crest. Suddenly I noticed the hitherto absent Dozy sitting over one of the letters of WEST PIER. In apparent irritation she chased off an offending crow and then did nothing more. It had been a fabulous afternoon's birdwatching.

Two days after that Dozy showed up in mid-afternoon when she flew straight to the Grand Hotel and perched on one of its balcony railings. First the Bedford, then the Metropole, and now an inspection of the Grand! Dozy had her reasons, however. Ropes and cradles temporarily straddled the Bedford Hotel and because of this, I thought, Dozy was inspecting alternative roosting sites. But, clearly, she could have no idea of the rates charged by the Grand. On the other hand, perhaps she did. For after a few minutes she left this select Brighton institution, never again to visit it while I was observing her, and proceeded to do some magnificent gliding around the pier though without ever seeming to do any serious chasing of pigeons. What little hunting there was that afternoon was provided by a sparrowhawk which had flown in to the pier in pursuit of starlings and then had left late in the afternoon treating watchers to a fascinating display of aerobatics high over the seafront's buildings. There was always something happening at the wonderful West Pier.

The afternoon of St Valentine's Day proved to be quite extraordinary. Braving the icy cold I arrived at the seafront early in the afternoon to be joined by John Reaney who suddenly spotted a kingfisher flying over the sea towards the pier. A kingfisher! It perched on a girder a few feet above the sea's surface, presumably with the intention of fishing, but any such intention was rudely dispelled by a herring gull which itself perhaps was on the lookout for a tasty meal. Pursued by the gull, the unfortunate kingfisher flew over the beach and boating pool, across Kings Road and into Regency Square where we lost sight of it. I think at least two drivers must have wondered what exactly that blue streak was which flashed past their windscreens! Not even the belated appearance of Dozy could compete with the unexpected presence of the kingfisher and she herself, after 15 minutes of unsuccessful pursuit of pigeons, soon disappeared into the pier just as a kestrel left it. Everything seemed to be retiring for the night so John and I, nearly frozen stiff, did the same.

A few days later Dozy did something I hadn't seen her do before. It had been a sunny afternoon but with a bitingly cold east wind. Suddenly Dozy appeared at about 5pm, warming my spirits, but after flying for only a few seconds she settled on a large pile of wood on the pier's east side to join a few pigeons and many hundreds of starlings. All very amicable, so it seemed, with peregrine, pigeons and starlings roosting together. However, the pigeons would have been well advised to leave immediately. Suddenly, with no apparent warning, Dozy leapt to one side and seized a pigeon. One nearby pigeon flew off but otherwise pigeons and starlings continued their tranquil roost as if nothing untoward had happened and Dozy proceeded to eat her meal. If it was this easy to grab a stationary pigeon, I wondered, why on earth does she do so much diving and chasing after pigeons on the wing? Because she enjoys it?

To my disappointment neither a lazy nor an energetic peregrine put in any appearance during the last days of February and I had to be content with watching the always magnificent starlings, three parties of brent geese flying from west to east over the sea, two shelducks and a pair of swans, and, of course, the faithful kestrels and sparrowhawks visiting the pier. Convinced that Dozy had left the pier to seek a mate elsewhere I wrote in my diary, "Good luck, old friend." I wrote it sadly. I had become very attached to this charismatic peregrine.

But I wasn't giving up on Dozy yet. It was, after all, only March. Three days into the month the afternoon was both sunny and windy – good Dozy flying conditions I thought hopefully – and, sure enough, when I arrived at the pier in mid-afternoon there indeed was my favourite peregrine perched in one of the pier's windows, 'dozing' as was her wont. Not that it mattered but it took this 'lazy' peregrine an hour to take to the wing and then it was only for some two minutes of superb flying before she retired again to her window to watch the world go by until the sun had set and she decided to turn in for the night. At top speed she flew to the Bedford Hotel to circle around it several times as if inspecting its annoying array of ropes and cradles and then evidently decided her favourite balcony was far too encumbered and settled instead on a ledge only some 20 feet over the then Restaurante Español at the junction of Preston Street and Kings Road. She really was very much an urban peregrine. Once again I wondered about her past. She seemed so much at home surrounded by people, houses and traffic.

Dozy was, of course, principally a pigeon fancier but by no means averse to a starling snack or two. On my next visit she did some spectacular flying, often jousting with the starlings and often surrounded by a huge cloud of them. Suddenly she simply seized one of them, took it to the deck of the pier, ate it, and within ten minutes was flying again. Just before her usual roost time she flew towards the Bedford Hotel and, despite the encumbrance of the various ropes and cradles, settled on her favourite balcony. Evidently the ledge above the Restaurante Español was not up to scratch.

The following two weeks were rather uneventful with Dozy usually present at the pier but doing little hunting, at least while I was watching. I began to suspect that my favourite avian lady had become a lazy carrion eater! Then on the afternoon of 20th March something happened that I will never forget. The tide was exceptionally low and John Reaney and I decided to walk to the sea's edge to get as close as we could to Dozy who was perched, as usual, over one of the letters of WEST PIER. Presumably the always observant falcon had come to expect our presence since at least one of us was usually present at the pier before sunset no matter what the weather and perhaps my reddish woolly hat was particularly distinctive. We saw Dozy apparently looking at her two admirers. Suddenly, to our great surprise and delight, she left her perch and began to fly low straight towards us. Presumably just a coincidence. But when she was almost exactly over our heads she turned round and flew back to her perch. Extraordinary! Would she have alighted on my (insufficiently protected) arm had I held it out horizontally? Just what had been the relationship, if any, between Dozy and people? I couldn't help but feel, despite trying hard to keep anthropomorphising tendencies under strict control!, that John and I had just been recipients of some sort of fraternal peregrine greeting. Needless to say, after Dozy's greeting to us, every other happening that afternoon seemed more than a little anticlimactic. A sparrowhawk unsuccessfully pursued a starling before dive-bombing majestically into the pier and then Dozy was also unsuccessful when it seemed far easier for her to catch a starling than avoid them all. Late in the day John and I rather reluctantly decided to head for home.

Dozy was absent the following afternoon but a charming black redstart loitered about the boating pool, five eider ducks floated out at sea, two sandwich terns flew past and, for good measure, a kestrel had a brief go at the assembled starlings.

The day of my next visit was dull, damp, drizzly and very windy. Horrible weather. I arrived late in the afternoon to see Dozy frantically chasing both starlings and pigeons without success. Once she dived from west of the Bedford Hotel as a party of six pigeons approached the pier flying over the sea also from the west. Dozy's sometime method – long recommended by me! – was to time her dive so that as she came up from the dive she would fly from behind and straight into unaware pigeons flying more or less in the same direction and thereby making it relatively easy for her to cling on to her quarry. In other words, no bouncing off. Timing was, of course, the essence. On this occasion Dozy came up from her dive a good ten yards ahead of the no doubt astonished pigeons. That afternoon she also used another tactic. Flying very fast from the pier towards the Bedford Hotel she would sometimes just suddenly turn round on a sixpence and reverse her direction, so flying very fast towards the pier. Presumably she hoped that way to take a pigeon by surprise but, if so, the tactic never worked. All that immense flying skill was to no avail. She eventually gave up and so did I a few minutes later.

Believing that Dozy had been in earnest the afternoon before but had retired for the night hungry, I went to the pier the following morning in the expectation of seeing a really determined Dozy in action. I saw no Dozy in action or otherwise. However, on returning at lunchtime there was Dozy floating high, high over the pier and then plunging down almost vertically towards it. Thrilling to say the least. I ran to a phone box to advise John to come immediately to the pier (no answer) and when I got back Dozy was in her favourite window vigorously plucking a pigeon, feathers flying in all directions. As to be expected, when I returned to the pier in the late afternoon Dozy was still in that very same window, looking very content, and she remained there, seemingly motionless, dozing, until I left two hours later.

The following afternoon Dozy was once again dozing in her favourite window but now my attention was focused on a glorious male wheatear feeding like a blackbird on one of the seafront's grass lawns. Each spring I look forward to seeing these handsome birds but I am always taken aback by just how gloriously handsome male wheatears are in their magnificent spring finery. If I were a female wheatear I would really get turned on. On my next visit Dozy was yet again in her favourite window, this time plucking a very alive pigeon and then enjoying her meal. Very gruesome indeed. The last days of March ended with Dozy always visible but doing nothing in particular. She was either in her favourite window or directly over one of the letters of WEST PIER, now nearly always the P, appropriately enough. How intelligent is this charismatic peregrine, I wondered!

April is a month for visiting other places but Dozy was often at the pier whenever I did manage a visit. Starling numbers were down to just a few hundred from the scores of thousands in the winter months but pigeon numbers remained the same. There were always pigeons for Dozy to pursue should she have been inclined. And towards the end of April she certainly did just that in what I wrote in my diary was an 'incredible and quite ferocious display'. When I arrived at the pier I immediately saw Dozy diving at pigeons from high over the Bedford or Metropole Hotels. On several occasions she was mobbed by two herring gulls and in retaliation tried to snatch at two different herring gulls minding their own business on the deck of the pier. After a dozen dives in some 20 minutes, each round trip thus taking about a minute and a half, Dozy took a breather for some 15 minutes and then she set off again. On her seventh dive luck and skill were on her side, for after being fiercely mobbed once again by the two herring gulls over the Bedford Hotel, she hit and hung on to a pigeon way out by the sea end of the pier. Drama was over for the afternoon and what drama.

The next four months were very busy ones for me with much travelling and various things to do. Moreover, I was beginning to take for granted my newfound friend at the West Pier. She would always be there, I thought, whenever I wanted to say hello. And, indeed, so she was throughout the summer. After autumn set in I decided once again to try to make at least one daily visit to that ornithological jewel of Brighton and Hove, the derelict West Pier.

And so I did but through September I saw Dozy only three times and once in early October when she suddenly appeared flying in and out of a flock of very agitated pigeons. The next few days were enlivened by the antics of visiting grey and pied wagtails. One morning I watched a grey wagtail feeding voraciously in the remaining puddles of the drained boating pool. It didn't take kindly to being disturbed. For when it was joined by another grey wagtail it chased the intruder far out to sea and then returned to feed in the pool. I was quite surprised by such unwarranted aggressive behaviour. However, three days later I saw two greys and one pied feeding amicably together. Presumably the pied was the peacemaker! After all, pied wagtails do roost together in their scores or even hundreds! By this time the pool's puddles had nearly dried up but the owner of a restaurant across the road allowed me to refill them using his tap water. It didn't seem proper to deprive the wagtails of the small puddles they so obviously relished. The following morning two pied and one grey were present in the pool, again without any skirmishing. However, my very suspect hypothesis that the pied is the peacemaker among wagtails was completely undone when a few mornings later I saw a feeding pied peremptorily chase away a visiting grey. It had been an enjoyable few days. In my opinion, wagtails are the most delightful of birds and it is always a great pleasure to see them. (My favourites are yellow wagtails but I had always to go to Arlington Reservoir to see them which I often did. There is surely not a more handsome bird in England than a male yellow wagtail in his full springtime grandeur. But then I also think that about springtime male wheatears....)

What of Dozy, however? I was really pleased to see the reappearance of my favourite feathered lady in the middle of October together with two sparrowhawks and, the following day, with a sparrowhawk and kestrel. Interestingly, I had never witnessed at the West Pier any sort of dispute between any of the raptors present. There seemed a live-and-let-live attitude between them. After all, they had no need to dispute over prey, of which there was always an abundance. But, as I was soon to discover, this was to change! I arrived one late afternoon to see Dozy, as I thought, sitting not on top of one of the letters of WEST PIER but, strangely, at the sea end of the pier. Was it my imagination or had Dozy shrunk in size? The penny dropped. This was not Dozy but another peregrine and a male one to boot! In great excitement I watched this new peregrine chase first pigeons and then starlings, all of them evading capture although one starling had to make a spectacular dive to inches above the waves to avoid its pursuer. But where was Dozy? Surely she hadn't deserted the pier because of the arrival of a male peregrine? On my second sighting of the new peregrine I watched him fly several times around the pier before disappearing beyond the high-rise building aptly named Sussex Heights. Evidently the new arrival was not roosting at the pier or on nearby hotels.

A few days later the male peregrine behaved in a way which enabled me to name him. When I arrived at the seafront I saw a kestrel and the male peregrine skirmishing together high over the pier before the kestrel managed to enter the pier, still, I noted, in one piece. A sparrowhawk then left the pier unmolested followed by another but when the kestrel left the pier it had to do so rather hurriedly, pursued yet again by the male peregrine which was calling loudly. What an aggressive male peregrine! I decided to call him Attila. November, I thought, promised to be a lot of fun if Attila took up residence at the pier. But why had Dozy left? Surely Attila had not driven her off. Would I ever see Dozy again, I wondered.

Certainly not through November. But Attila didn't disappoint. He gave incredible flying displays involving very fast stoops and, unlike Dozy, would occasionally pursue pigeons around Sussex Heights although he seemed to have great difficulty in catching any. Starlings, however, were an entirely different matter. Early on I saw him catch a starling high in the air and then take it out to sea for several minutes, slowly losing height all the time, before returning to the pier to consume his meal. He even seemed to enjoy plunging into swirling clouds of starlings and once I saw him stoop downwards at great speed before turning upwards and simply disappearing into a huge mass of very agitated starlings. Certainly he was a most aggressive male peregrine and what he lacked in size compared to Dozy he seemed to make up for in aggression. Once again a kestrel had to beat a hasty retreat simply because it was apparently in the wrong place at the wrong time. Moreover, on several occasions I saw him attack herring gulls just for the fun of it, as it appeared to me, and I often wondered what he would do should he ever impale one. On another occasion two carrion crows made the serious mistake of mobbing Attila but when he turned on them they very quickly and very wisely decided they had more urgent matters to attend to. Surely, I thought, this was a male capable enough to partner the charismatic Dozy. But where was she? Why had she vanished at about the same time Attila had appeared? It made no sense to me.

My regret at the disappearance of Dozy only increased when Attila was mysteriously absent for a week. However, on the day the pier had survived a fierce assault from a Channel gale I was doubly relieved to see Attila patrolling the battered framework as if to protect it from further harm and, moreover, obviously determined to do some serious hunting. When he made a very spectacular kill of a pigeon, his first of a pigeon I'd seen thus far, I thought yet again that Attila would make a very capable partner for Dozy. If only she would return and give him a courting chance. Just two days later my wish was granted or at least the first part was.

I arrived on 10th December, quite early in the afternoon, to see Dozy high over the Bedford Hotel. To say that I was delighted would be an understatement. In typical Dozy fashion she made five spectacular dives towards the pier, went round it at speed and then returned to high over the hotel. I was very surprised when instead of performing a sixth dive she suddenly flew like a bullet towards the Metropole Hotel, straight towards, I saw in astonishment, another peregrine but one considerably smaller than herself, Attila! If this was an amorous advance, however, it was not of the most subtle and Attila – just where had he come from? – could have been forgiven for thinking otherwise. At any rate Dozy appeared to collide with Attila, there was a brief skirmish, they locked talons and both fell spiralling towards the roof of the Metropole, disengaging only just before hitting the roof and disappearing from my sight. I waited anxiously for a long time for at least one of the peregrines to resurface but I waited in vain. Somewhat concerned for their safety, I went home wondering just what it was I had witnessed: the first move initiated by the lady in what was to be a beautiful romance or an unambiguous declaration by her of eternal hostility? I hoped that soon I would come to understand at least a little about the subtleties of peregrine courtship.

Still rather concerned, I visited the pier next day both in the morning and at lunchtime. No peregrine was present. I returned again early in the afternoon and eventually my patience was rewarded. Suddenly not only was a kestrel high over the pier but also Dozy. A few minutes later the kestrel flew off and Dozy also disappeared from view somewhere towards the sea end of the pier. Glancing towards Sussex Heights I was astonished to see a small peregrine flying past the building which I took to be Attila. So both Dozy and Attila were fine. But had Dozy hidden, I wondered, because she had seen Attila at the skyscraper? No matter, with Attila safely gone Dozy re-emerged to treat all watchers to a stunning display of flying and hunting though without any success and in the end she flew off in the direction of the marina. It seemed that, for whatever the reason, Dozy no longer roosted at the pier or on the Bedford Hotel.

My hopes of a rapprochement between Dozy and Attila, even of a possible courtship, were not to be realised, at least not in 1994 for I had no more sightings of Dozy though Attila made quite a few appearances. Just before Christmas he spectacularly chased a few pigeons and then tried a new tactic of waiting menacingly under the huge mass of starlings for one of them to 'panic' and to try to reach the safety of the pier. However, when on the two occasions one of them did just that, the diving, twisting, turning starling somewhat easily, I thought, managed to evade the talons and beak of the pursuing Attila. On Boxing Day a kestrel, while being vigorously mobbed by starlings, hovered over the beach end of the pier while Attila did some more spectacular hunting and, in keeping with his character, aggressively saw off an offending herring gull. A really fascinating year's peregrine watching was nicely rounded off on the penultimate day of the year when Attila flew to a great height and simply dived at breakneck speed straight into an alarmingly huge conglomeration of starlings. A most inadvisable and dangerous undertaking, I thought, certainly not a hunting technique I recommended in any way, and I looked long and hard for another sighting of that small, aggressive male peregrine. Not a glimpse of him, nor on the 31st. The disturbing sight of him diving fiercely into that huge, pulsating mass of starlings had been my final slighting of him in 1994. As far as I knew, the scores of thousands of flying little black shapes had just swallowed him whole the day before. Yet, deep down, I knew that Attila would quickly resurface in 1995.

1995: A Year of Peregrine Consolidation

And so it proved. The New Year began in a most pleasing way with two sparrowhawks frolicking together at the end of the pier and the reckless Attila emerging from his 31st December absence to reassure watchers with a ten-minute spell of typical Attila-style hunting. A few days later, despite a bitterly cold wind lashing the seafront, things really hotted up, ornithologically speaking. I arrived after lunch and before long Attila appeared as if from nowhere and to my astonishment chased a lone starling around the pier for some five minutes without ever getting close to catching it. He eventually gave up and flew to high over the Bedford

Hotel from where he surveyed the huge, high flock of thousands of starlings which had by that time gathered over the pier. A standoff occurred. Then the entire flock charged Attila who somewhat ignominiously retreated, only allowing himself to return to his original 'floating' position after the triumphant starling flock had returned to its original position. Astonishingly, this apparent humiliation of Attila was repeated several times before Attila, having presumably lost patience, made as if to charge the disrespectful starling horde which then split up, in apparent panic, into several frantic sub-hordes before regrouping and, with order restored, as I watched incredulously, proceeded to charge Attila again. After about half an hour of such thrilling jousting Attila disappeared behind the sea end of the pier and I left, frozen stiff but thrilled to bits. Birdwatching at its thrilling best, I thought to myself. But what on earth was all that jousting really about?

From then on Attila was always visible at the pier, aggressive as usual, now seeing off sparrowhawks as well as kestrels. When in the middle of January I saw Attila hit a pigeon at great speed following a very high dive, the pigeon just bounced, as was often the case, and flew off. Try to catch a pigeon surreptitiously from behind was my constant advice to Attila, as it had been to Dozy, but of course it was always possible that, when stooping, neither peregrine was seriously hunting but just enjoying the thrill of the dive. In any case, I would have been immensely disappointed had either taken my advice!

The 19th January was the atrocious day I referred to earlier when I battled my way to the pier just to see whether the starlings would arrive or not. And arrive they did, these magnificent, fantastic starlings, but no aerobatics that afternoon, straight down into the refuge to dry out, get warm, and no doubt to have a prolonged natter about the impossible weather.

The weather the following day was temporarily much better – it could hardly have been worse – and after I arrived at the pier I soon saw that incoming starlings were resuming their inexplicable behaviour, interrupted for just one day. By the time Attila arrived an immensely large number of them were already swirling high over the pier. Almost immediately the huge flock charged and recharged Attila but completely panicked when Attila flew straight into their midst only for him to emerge with nothing to show for his daring, if, of course, he had been seeking a meal rather than just a thrill. Finally, after about 15 minutes and certainly empty-handed, Attila himself left the jousting arena when his sparring partners apparently decided they had had enough of peregrine fun and games for one evening and descended to the pier to roost. This meant that some starlings had been flying for about an hour and a half and most of them for well over an hour. The enigma remains: why do they do it and why don't they all go to ground as soon as any raptor arrives, let alone an aggressive male peregrine? Had Attila arrived simply in order to enjoy the jousting, with little or even no intention of having a meal? The winds were still strong, clouds were looking very menacing, and bolts of lighting flashed a foreboding message out at sea. Reluctantly I left the derelict West Pier and its wild environs to another tempestuous night.

Sure enough, gale force winds and rain did not abate till after lunch next day and when I arrived at the seafront Attila was already floating high over the Bedford Hotel but not a single starling was cavorting over its night-time abode. Some 15 minutes later an obviously impatient Attila flew inland leaving me on my own, a bit puzzled, to await the arrival of the first starlings. Presumably they were a little late because the atrocious weather conditions of the morning had delayed their departure. At any rate, seemingly enjoying the windy conditions, the starlings, once they had arrived, danced together as usual until late in the afternoon when almost of one accord they descended to the West Pier to spend what would surely be another restless night.

The 24th January proved a landmark day at the West Pier, the day I had been waiting for! The afternoon was dry, dull and breezy, perfect conditions for some good birdwatching, and it wasn't long before the daily starling partying was in full swing. Two sparrowhawks and a kestrel arrived as habitual gatecrashers before the starlings began to go to roost. Suddenly a pair of peregrines, a male and female, appeared from behind the sea end of the pier, the female almost immediately disappearing behind the front of the pier from whence she'd come while the male flew about for a few minutes, indulging in a passing lunge at the remaining starlings. A male and female at the pier and apparently getting on together. Dozy and Attila? Surely not Dozy, she had never 'hidden' behind the sea end of the pier. But it could well have been Attila. In deepening gloom and beginning drizzle I nevertheless returned home elated.

The following afternoon was dull, damp and again breezy and when I arrived at the seafront it was with a very expectant feeling. Twenty minutes' wait and the first starlings arrived and 15 minutes after that who should suddenly arrive at the pier but Dozy! Immediately she jousted with the starlings, lunged at a herring gull, then hunted non-stop in her spectacular characteristic way until she flew off eastwards five minutes after the starlings had begun to roost. Would Attila show up? I waited another 15 minutes but then decided that a warm flat has very undeniable attractions.

Normally when I visit Norfolk I am not at all anxious to return to Brighton but on this occasion I was. And eight days later or, better, one rough-legged buzzard, four common cranes and many marsh and hen harriers later (thanks to my brother Chris), I was back in Brighton in early February and immediately at the seafront to see a male peregrine disappear behind the sea end of the pier. Had it been Attila? Was I even sure it was a male? A few visits later I noticed at the sea end of the pier a single peregrine on the lookout while perched on one of two diagonal wires running from the top of a high mast to the pier's deck below. This peregrine's behaviour was quite novel. When it took to the wing it did two fast flights not only around the pier but under its structure as well. No other peregrine had ever done this. I was sure it wasn't Dozy. A different peregrine, the female of 24th January? After its two most unusual flights this third peregrine perched on a railing and was occupied in meticulous preening when I left. The following afternoon I again saw this new peregrine on the lookout from the same diagonal wire as before but after just a few minutes it took to the wing and I was in for a treat. Immediately the peregrine began to joust with the assembled starlings until one of them dropped from the great height to which the assembled mass had risen and tried to reach the safety of the pier. And reach it the starling did, almost seeming to mock the peregrine as this most fearsome of raptors tried unsuccessfully to make continual grabs at its elusive quarry. More fantastic jousting, then one starling broke ranks and flew in the direction of Sussex Heights, this time not pursued by the peregrine. Several times the peregrine was completely submerged in the cloud of twisting, turning, panicking starlings but eventually, after emerging starling-less every time, it came into view triumphantly carrying a starling in its talons and promptly disappeared with it. All that effort for just one measly, skinny, scrawny starling. But what a fantastic afternoon's birdwatching it had been.

Needless to say, I could hardly wait to see again this new peregrine but success eluded me. Even on a lovely, sunny afternoon, with my hopes thus raised, I was just about to leave when I suddenly saw a peregrine flying over the pier. I recognised her immediately. It was Dozy! For half an hour she did her characteristic fabulous diving and then she flew off and I trudged homewards, happy to have seen my favourite lady peregrine once again. Had I known then that that afternoon of 12th February 1995 would be the last time I would ever set eyes on Dozy, it would have been, on the contrary, a very mournful, wistful birdwatcher trudging homewards thinking about all the good times he had enjoyed with Dozy but never to be repeated.

Attila, a pair of unidentified peregrines, Dozy, an unidentified single peregrine, Dozy again – I was puzzled. What was happening at the West Pier?

Despite several subsequent visits to the pier, it was not until the end of February that one afternoon I saw an unidentified peregrine fly into the pier where it remained motionless till I left. However, I did see some action that day for in the morning I had seen a dolphin periodically surfacing only some 20 yards from the shore. Every so often there's a real surprise at the marvellous West Pier.

Now convinced that there would be no pair of peregrines at the pier that spring, I wasn't too concerned about making daily visits and when I did eventually visit an ever reliable sparrowhawk was present but no peregrine. One March morning I saw a brent goose glide on to the Hove lawns where it fed and rested until lunchtime when I left. Presumably there was something wrong with it; perhaps the goose was very tired or even injured. However, it was not on the lawns when I returned after lunch, neither could I see any peregrine at the pier.

April is such a good month for visiting other excellent locations that it wasn't until the end of the third week that I was gazing once more at the incomparable West Pier. Starlings began to arrive in the early evening, quickly building up numbers to about 2000, and then suddenly I saw a smallish peregrine spectacularly chasing them, only taking time off for occasional irritable forays at herring gulls. Surely this was Attila. If it was, I saw him again on three more visits and finally when he hunted for a few minutes before streaking off over the Metropole Hotel.

Most of May was taken up with a visit to Norfolk and a birdwatching trip abroad, so that by the time June arrived I was more than anxious to see what was happening at the West Pier though I was reasonably sure that from now on peregrines would never entirely desert the pier. Sure enough, when I arrived one evening in early June I noticed straightaway a large peregrine, therefore a female, busily preening herself on one of the pier's railings. I decided to name her, in the expectation and hope that she would be a semi-permanent resident just as Dozy had been. For no good reason I decided on Sophie. Hoping to see a little action from Sophie I returned the following three evenings and to my great surprise I saw her the first two times in exactly the same place and, more often than not, enjoying a good preen and the third time she was again perched on a railing. But there was no action. During my next visit I suddenly saw a peregrine flying round the pier and being harassed by two considerably bigger herring gulls. Such a small peregrine must obviously be a male, I thought, but it clearly wasn't Attila since that aggressive little peregrine would never have tolerated such indignities. After settling once over the letters WEST PIER, something in any case I'd never seen Attila do, he disappeared behind the sea end of the pier, presumably to look out to sea. Three evenings later it was, I thought, Sophie who was perched on one of the pier's railings. But the following evening I was sure it was the new male which I saw flying far out to sea, then circling high in the sky for some ten minutes before returning to perch on one of the pier's two diagonal 'lookout' wires as a prelude to disappearing for the night. I was a little irritated with myself, I had lost track of what was happening at the pier.

The summer then went by and it wasn't until the end of September that I began to visit the West Pier again on a regular basis. What would I find? First of all, I saw Attila – yes, I'm sure it was Attila! – catch a pigeon and to show that achievement was no fluke the following day he caught one of those so elusive starlings. Next there were two peregrines at the pier but, apparently, not together as a couple. For me, the autumn had never truly begun until I had seen a pied wagtail at the front and this happy event occurred on 13th October. Late in October I witnessed my first raptor dispute of the winter when the aggressive Attila attacked a lone kestrel but the following afternoon Attila did not attack when two kestrels turned up together. However, exactly 24 hours later Attila once more fiercely attached a lone visiting kestrel. Attila was certainly aggressive though perhaps not too brave – a typical bully! But perhaps this male was not Attila. In early November there were again two peregrines at the pier but, as before, not obviously together as a couple. I next enjoyed watching a sparrowhawk and a detachment of starlings jousting together magnificently and then watching three kestrels, two sparrowhawks and a peregrine at the pier without any altercations – perhaps because the peregrine was outnumbered and, in any case, was too busy catching a pigeon. Moreover, this peregrine was a bit on the large size for a male and I assumed she was female. Was she Sophie? There was no way to tell. The following day I saw her swoop on a scoter duck, three days later she again caught a pigeon and the next day she gave chase to a crow as if she really meant to catch it. She would most certainly be a fitting partner for Attila! But where was Attila? In mid-November at long last I saw a male and female peregrine amicably perched together almost side by side on the pier, definitely a couple! Attila and Sophie? And they were still amicably together when I arrived the following day. Excellent! However, only one peregrine was present on my next visit when it chased and, I think, caught an unfortunate wader far out to sea. A day later and more normal service was resumed when one of the two residing peregrines caught a starling after a spectacular dive. On my next visit I saw two sparrowhawks, two kestrels and two peregrines with, surprisingly, no altercations of any kind.

Whenever I was thus lulled into thinking that the various raptors at the pier had at last learned to co-exist or, rather, that the peregrines had finally decided they would have to share the pier with fellow raptors, I was quickly proved wrong. So after arriving at the seafront to see a peregrine perched on one of the pier's railings, just a little later I witnessed, to my astonishment, a kind of gentlemen's duel between a sparrowhawk and a second peregrine. High over the Metropole Hotel each raptor took it in turns to dive on the other until finally, after four or five dives each, the peregrine soared to a great height and stooped fiercely down on the sparrowhawk which, I think wisely, decided to abandon the fun and games. Deprived of his or her play-mate, the peregrine floated off eastwards. Suddenly a third peregrine joined the first on the pier railing – the couple together again. By the time I left for home, I was more than a bit confused over what I had seen. Surely the sparrowhawk and peregrine had been playfully sparring together until the sparrowhawk took umbrage at the peregrine's over-zealous stoop? Perhaps they were both juveniles practising their stooping skills?

On one of my last November visits a pair of peregrines were still present at the pier with the female chasing and catching a pigeon and the male successively dive-bombing two sparrowhawks. The next day a pair of peregrines were again present and, to my surprise, were joined by another female. Three peregrines perched amicably together! I really don't understand the behaviour of peregrines. On the last morning of the year (having been away a month) I visited the West Pier and was immensely pleased to see a pair of peregrines present and to watch one of them, seemingly effortlessly, catching a pigeon in straight flight.

1996: The Peregrines Need Help

After a New Year's trip to Norfolk I was once more extremely pleased to see the pair of peregrines still in residence at the West Pier and even more pleased to see them display-ing to each other. They were very much a courting couple. On one absorbing day the male chased the female for a while and the female chased and caught a starling, perhaps demonstrating to the male what he ought to be doing. Ten days into February the female showed her versatility with a fantastic display of flying, ending with a pigeon as a trophy. The following day, not to be outdone, the male put on a spectacular display, closely observed, if not admiringly by his partner, then certainly by me. Indeed, watching peregrines at the West Pier had become more interesting than ever. On my next visit the female gave enthralling chase to pigeons, though eventually had to make do with a lowly starling and again for much of the time she was pursued, or perhaps just followed, by the male. Two days later the female did catch a pigeon after which she and her partner put on a thrilling display of togetherness. The following day the male and female joined forces to see off a luckless sparrowhawk but, strangely, paid no attention to two visiting kestrels. On my last February visit I saw them watching a herring gull continually attacking one of two razorbills swimming near to the pier. Since now at least one of the two peregrines was always present at the pier and often both of them, it seemed not improbable to me that they would try to breed somewhere close by or perhaps even on the pier itself.

March opened with just one peregrine at the pier and a very elegant red-throated diver swimming and, of course, diving nearby. When, I wondered, would I see the two peregrines mate or would they mate only if they had already found a secure enough nesting site to their satisfaction? On the 10th day of the month I watched, heart in mouth, as the female flew high to the east to intercept a lapwing flying westwards over the sea. I had grown up with lapwings on the Norfolk coast and they remain one of my most loved birds, so that I was definitely rooting for the lapwing as it twisted, turned and successfully dodged every deadly lunge made by the peregrine. Finally, after several minutes of this ferocious but frustrated endeavour, the falcon abandoned her still very much alive dinner and the lapwing continued unmolested on its westward course but looking decidedly groggy and disorientated. If only the male had gone to help his partner, then surely the lapwing would have become a meal for one or both of them. I was pleased he had remained only a spectator. In any case, I reflected, I had never seen the peregrines cooperating together in a hunt.

This was remedied some days later when both peregrines hunted pigeons together, one taking over as soon as the other temporarily gave up the chase. Nevertheless, even in taking turns to hunt, the peregrines did not succeed in catching their quarry. One really has to admire theses feral pigeons. Of course, they are flying for their lives whereas the peregrines are flying only for a meal and perhaps, who knows, hunting only for the fun of it or sometimes only going through the motions. But that afternoon the hunting seemed deadly serious to me.

The next red-letter day was on 26th March when six sparkling wheatears were at the seafront (four males and two females) and, very unexpectedly, 22 great-crested grebes were floating out at sea. Excitedly I returned to the front at noon the following day to see only three wheatears but the number of grebes had risen to 43! Four hours later I counted 59 grebes in three distinct groups of 28, 23, and 8. Extraordinary! And there was now a pair of peregrines at the pier. Two days later, again in the late afternoon, I saw one male wheatear at the front and 29 grebes on the sea. During the last two days of the month the pair of peregrines were once more at the pier and in addition the environs of the boating pool were enriched by the presence of a lovely female black redstart. But the grebes had vanished.

The redstart, however, was still present into April and obviously enjoying some welcome early spring sunshine. Of the peregrines there was now no sign. Ought I to be doing something, I wondered, to try to protect them, more specifically, to provide them with a secure breeding site somewhere? One night I had a really horrible nightmare. Pursued by an enormous, relentless kestrel, I woke up in a sweat, heart pounding, just as the raptor was about to strike at me. Why a kestrel? I had clearly identified my pursuer as a kestrel and not a peregrine. Thank goodness it wasn't a peregrine! Had it been a peregrine, who knows what might have happened! Next day, with that vengeful kestrel still very much on my mind, I went to the pier and was pleased to see once again the pair of peregrines present. Determined to try to help them, I returned home and phoned, as it then was, English Nature in Lewes to ask if this Government Conservation Agency would do something to facilitate successful breeding for the West Pier peregrines. Since special permission had then to be obtained from English Nature even to approach a peregrine's nest site, this seemed the logical thing to do. But the response was that English Nature could and would take action only if the peregrines were actually breeding. I then phoned the headquarters of the RSPB for the southeast of England, based in Brighton. No, it seemed, nothing would be done unless the peregrines were actually breeding. Catch 22! I remember feeling really quite bewildered about why nothing was to be done to provide the peregrines with a secure nest site. I just didn't' think the peregrines could breed successfully in what was essentially a starling and pigeon roost, even if they were able to find a suitable spot. They would attempt to breed, I thought, on a hotel ledge but I doubted that they would succeed. I resolved to keep a lookout. In four more visits to the pier I saw each time only a single peregrine but on 10th April I saw not only the pair of peregrines but the pair were doing what a courting pair of peregrines ought to be doing – they were copulating, albeit with the female perched precariously on one of the pier's two diagonal wires, after which both of them took off in what seemed like a celebratory flight around the pier. This was certainly firm evidence of at least breeding intentions and once again I phoned the Brighton-based RSPB regional headquarters and once again the response was negative. Of course, it was all too easy for me to believe that limited local resources could be stretched just enough to include the construction and erection of a peregrine nestbox!

Before the week had passed I saw the two peregrines mate once more, and two days later I saw them display their 'togetherness' by hunting in unison for a whole hour but with all pigeons somehow or other managing to evade capture, though one was knocked to the deck of the pier from which it flew off, apparently unscathed. On subsequent visits to the pier I saw only one peregrine and I hoped that its partner was incubating eggs somewhere nearby. However, on an evening visit to the pier at the end of the month I saw both peregrines together and took this to mean, perhaps somewhat prematurely, that the peregrines were not breeding.

During the summer months I made few visits to the seafront and only began regular visits again in October when I was very pleased to see a pair of peregrines still patrolling the West Pier. About a month after that something very spectacular happened. Both the peregrines were on the pier when John Reaney and I saw in the distance a short-eared owl approaching the coast from over the sea. The luckless owl never made terra firma. The female peregrine flew straight towards it and for several minutes a dogfight ensued which ended in the owl doing an about turn and retreating away from the shore and back out to sea. I felt very sorry for it and wondered what would be its fate. I feared, I hope needlessly, a watery one. In *Macbeth* an old man relates during most 'unnatural' times how 'a falcon, towering in her pride of place, was by a mousing owl hawk'd at and kill'd'. Evidently in Brighton and Hove on the day of 9th November 1996 everything had been and remained entirely natural!

From then until the end of the year there were nearly always visiting kestrels and sparrowhawks at the West Pier but usually only one of the two peregrines. On Christmas Day I was surprised to see a heron fly past the pier and unmolested by any peregrine. Ominously for the peregrines, a walkway had been constructed during December linking the shore with the hitherto isolated concert hall and pier head which meant that the West Pier Trust would in future be able to take paying parties of people on conducted tours of the pier. Indeed, over 2000 people were taken on these tours through 1997. Eventually the entire pier was to be restored. Perhaps welcomed by one and all was the pier's re-illumination in December, with the letters WEST PIER lit up by some 250 light bulbs. The Grand Old Lady was now shining forth to everyone her need and desire for resurrection. As if in defiance of the odds steadily mounting against them, on the very last day of the year the pair of peregrines patrolled their once trusty sanctuary for at least an hour. The West Pier belonged to them and not to the West Pier Trust.

1997: The Peregrines' West Pier Under Siege

The peregrines' defiance continued into New Year's Day since the two of them were still clearly visible at the pier during the last hour of daylight. A visiting kestrel went unmolested. However, the following day with workers now present in the pier head the peregrines were conspicuously absent. Nevertheless, the kestrel put in another visit though even that elegant raptor went temporarily absent as work in the pier inexorably continued. In mid-January I saw the female peregrine arrive to circle the pier just once, no doubt to check on what was happening. From then on there were usually one or two kestrels visiting at sunset together with an occasional sparrowhawk but I saw no peregrine at any time during the next two weeks. However, a visit by one of the two peregrines at the end of the month presaged their triumphant February return, not to take up residence again in the West Pier but on, to the peregrines, the virtually adjacent skyscraper of Sussex Heights. They would use the West Pier whenever those pesky but basically harmless two-legged, unfeathered creatures were not swarming all over their former residence but otherwise they would survey the seafront and sea from their various lookout posts on Sussex Heights and fly their sorties from its favoured balconies.

Thus, two days into February, I arrived at the seafront about an hour before sunset and noticed straightaway the male peregrine on top of Sussex Heights and his partner perched on a balcony railing a few floors below. Shortly afterwards they both began hunting in spectacular fashion. After expertly catching a starling the male dropped it to his partner who deftly caught it and then carried it around for a minute or so before in turn simply dropping it into empty space! To my very great astonishment, the much abused starling then flew straight back to the sanctuary of the West Pier! If this was a present spurned, the male peregrine took no offence for both then hunted a pigeon together, sometimes both of them only a foot or two from their quarry which nevertheless, twisting and turning, managed to evade its two pursuers and reach the safety of the pier. Incredible! What a magnificent pigeon! But the spectacle was not yet over. The male peregrine next went solo on a sustained and relentless pursuit of starlings but with no success at all. I wondered if any starlings caught would once again be passed to the female. Perhaps this is what she expected because when the defeated male retired to Sussex Heights, the female also landed and rested for a time on the pier, then took off in pursuit of pigeons, caught one in her very first swoop and despite being aggressively mobbed by a crow took her catch to the end of the pier and ate her dinner in full view. The sun was now setting on what had been a scintillating, fascinating spectacle.

On my next two visits to the West Pier both peregrines were again present though without doing any hunting. Never mind, I told myself, they were obviously not going to desert the West Pier or the convenient high-rise buildings alongside or near to the shoreline, especially, of course, Sussex Heights. Yet it was to be at the end of February when I next saw a peregrine at the pier and this one didn't linger but quickly flew off in the direction of the marina. It seemed to me the peregrines were not at all happy that parties of people were now regularly being taken on tours of the full length of the pier. Perhaps the safety helmets visitors were required to wear were a safeguard not so much against falling timber as against irate peregrines! At any rate, a few visits later I again saw a single peregrine on the pier and then again in mid-March when two unique events happened: a visiting kestrel gratuitously attacked the peregrine and a sparrowhawk aborted its stoop into the pier, again for no apparent reason. However, it was on the following day that a most remarkable incident happened. John Reaney and I watched a peregrine catch a pigeon – nothing too unusual there – but in order to try to avoid mobbing by a herring gull the peregrine flew out to sea with its prey, nevertheless still closely pursued by the remorseless gull which, to our surprise, succeeded in making the peregrine drop its booty into the sea. To our even greater surprise, the hapless pigeon was not only still alive but managed to row some 20 to 30 yards to the pier using its wings as oars! Whether it succeeded in clambering up the girders to relative safety we were not able to see. I feared not. But I decided I admire starlings and feral pigeons just as much as I do peregrines!

This was just as well for on my next ten or so visits to the pier there were no peregrines to admire, just starlings and pigeons, with usually a visiting sparrowhawk and kestrel. Though I was not able to make any visits through April, early in May I was delighted to see a pair of peregrines back at the pier. Both of them were still making use of Sussex Heights and, moreover, in mid-May I saw for the first time a peregrine on a balcony of Chartwell Court, a high-rise building of flats facing Sussex Heights. Better still, the following day I saw a pair of peregrines on different balconies of Chartwell Court, the female, however, clearly immature. I was sure that if a nestbox were erected in any suitable place on Chartwell Court or Sussex Heights then peregrines would breed in the spring next year, the maturity of the female permitting. In the middle of June Peter Whitcomb phoned me about the possibility of the Sussex Ornithological Society (the SOS) erecting just such a nestbox and that same evening I watched a pair of peregrines continuing to use Sussex Heights as a base for their various sorties. Things therefore seemed to be proceeding very nicely!

Through the following four months at least one peregrine, often two, could be seen flying to and from both Sussex Heights and the West Pier. Unusual incidents continued to happen. One day in September a peregrine was perched on the parapet of the north side of Sussex Heights (I liked to call this side the 'north face'), seemingly minding its own business, when a sparrowhawk on its way to the West Pier swooped down on the peregrine and pulled out of its dive only a foot or so above the peregrine's head. The aristocratic peregrine deigned not even to notice! Yet sparrowhawks were certainly not always that bold – or foolhardy. Once in October a party of a mere hundred or so starlings charged an approaching sparrowhawk and put it totally to flight; the sparrowhawk didn't just retreat temporarily, it turned tail and disappeared from sight. But I was no longer much interested in the sunset battles of starlings and sparrowhawks. What I wanted was a pair of peregrines to be in residence in the crucial first months of 1998.

So, after returning from a long birdwatching holiday in the middle of November, the first thing I did was to check on the peregrines and to my relief I immediately saw both male and female on the West Pier and, better still, a few days later I was treated to a delightful peregrine 'pas de deux'. Moreover, not only were the peregrines continuing to use the West Pier but, more importantly from a breeding point of view, also the balconies of Sussex Heights. Things were therefore continuing to proceed very nicely! Even so, it was still reassuring to see just before Christmas both male and female at the seafront, the male perched on the pier and the female on her favourite balcony railing of Sussex Heights. However, despite almost daily visits till the end of the year I saw no more peregrines. That was unexpected. I couldn't help feeling just a little worried.

1998: The Year of the Sussex Heights Nestbox.

Of course, I needn't have worried. Nevertheless, after returning from Norfolk in early January, I was certainly relieved to see both peregrines still in residence and very much 'in form'. On 12th January, after I'd witnessed spectacular hunting displays by both male and female, I was convinced the female actually tried to catch a visiting sparrowhawk! Perhaps, though, she was just being even more exuberant than usual. Significantly, on 15th January I saw once again a peregrine perched on top of the north face of Sussex Heights, a superb lookout post, a mere 330 feet or so high! If there was any one place, I thought, suitable for a nestbox, it was there. However, the peregrines' favourite location continued to be the West Pier and, on Sussex Heights, the sea-facing railing of a much favoured apartment. Apparently, the peregrines had chosen this particular apartment because the occupant had long been absent but at the end of the month I had to chuckle when I saw an undoubtedly very indignant gentleman hard at work cleaning up an accumulated mass of pigeon and other carcasses and, no doubt, accompanied by myriads of very fat maggots! Thereafter the railing was festooned with various paraphernalia to try to deter the peregrines from future usage. But balconies were not in short supply on Sussex Heights!

Throughout February the pair of peregrines continued to be present and at the end of the month I saw them not only displaying together but on three separate occasions chasing together a herring gull, apparently just for the fun of it. Their behaviour was most encouraging. But when would the SOS erect the so necessary nestbox? Early in March Peter Whitcomb wrote to me to say that Graham Roberts, a professional ecologist and Portsmouth-based member of the SOS, had not only erected a peregrine nestbox on Chichester Cathedral in 1995 (then still unoccupied) but was now spending a great deal of his obviously limited free time in trying to arrange the erection of a nestbox on a suitable site in Brighton. This was wonderful news. On 10th March Graham and I spoke over the phone and we agreed to meet just three days later in front of the West Pier. I relayed the good news to John Reaney and the two of us met Graham at the seafront as arranged, both of us willing the peregrines to put on a good morning show. And put on a good show they did. Graham was very impressed! I for my part was more than impressed at the enormous amount of work Graham had single-handedly already done and John and I stressed the suitability of Sussex Heights as a nestbox location for the peregrines. Graham moved incredibly swiftly. Just six days later I received a letter from him saying that he had obtained permission to erect a box at the top of the north face of Sussex Heights and not only had he already inspected the site but a local building firm was constructing a nestbox from his design and, all being well, would fix the box under his guidance on 23rd March. Word spread quickly. The local newspaper, *The Argus*, printed an article about the impending erection of the nestbox with the excellent news that this was now to become a joint SOS/ RSPB project. If, I thought, only another peregrine could match the speed of a peregrine in a stoop, it seemed the natural order of things that only another peregrine-devoted aficionado could even have kept Graham Roberts in sight in these last crucial days! I fervently hoped the peregrines would show their appreciation in the desired way. I was sure they would.

On 23rd March the nestbox was duly erected to the accompaniment that afternoon of an *Argus* photograph showing Graham checking the box's position on the top of Sussex Heights. Local television also featured the thrilling event. There was a persistent rumour that Graham had left a user's manual in the box! We all waited with baited breath. At 3pm that afternoon I saw the pair of peregrines on the pier and in a visit two hours later they were still there. Presumably the peregrines would not have taken kindly to the humans' invasion of their Sussex Heights territory but, on the other hand, as soon as they had sussed out what those pesky trespassers had somehow or other construed to leave behind.... Once again the peregrines were at the pier when I checked everything the following afternoon. But I was encouraged to see the male peregrine displaying over the female who was perched, as usual, on one of the pier's two diagonal lookout wires. However, I was disappointed at the total lack of response shown by the female. Not only did she not meet her mate on one of his dives, turn over on her back and lock talons with him (as apparently required of a turned-on female!), but even when the male finally landed only inches from her side she remained frustratingly unimpressed. At any rate, no mating ensued. Next day after morning rain I checked

56

Plate 1   The letters WEST PIER illuminated in December 1996.

Plate 2   View of the pre-2003 West Pier showing the walkway built in
December 1996. The entire pier was criminally set alight and
destroyed in the spring of 2003.

Plate 3 & 4   Two views of the burnt-out West Pier, post-2003, showing
wintering and still loyal starlings massing overhead.

Plate 5   Graham Roberts installing the nestbox on 23rd March 1998, with Chartwell Court in the background.

Plate 6   View of Sussex Heights from the top of Chartwell Court showing the peregrine nestbox on the top of the 'north face'. The West Pier, pre-2003, is visible behind the Metropole Hotel.

Plate 7 Three peregrine chicks, about nine days old, admiring their handsome father!

Plate 8 Three decidedly ugly 'ducklings'!

Plate 9   Three peregrine chicks about 20 days old, perhaps not yet at their most beautiful!

Plate 10   A juvenile female peregrine, about 45 days old, poses for the
camera on a 20th-floor balcony of Sussex Heights. Who will
blink first, the peregrine or the photographer?

the peregrines' whereabouts and was more than delighted, almost ecstatic, to see both of them on top of the north face of Sussex Heights. Moreover, after a short flight, the female returned to the top of the north face, ate something, and then perched just a yard or so from the box, seemingly on guard! There she was at lunchtime the following day, 26th March, and two hours later I saw either her or the male still on the parapet of the north face. Most excitingly of all, a fellow birdwatcher, Chris Phillips, told me that later in the afternoon he had seen the female actually enter the nestbox! But would she understand what it was there for? The following afternoon, the fourth day after the nestbox's erection, I saw the female once again standing guard by the box while her mate was perched at the pier; then he flew to the top of Sussex Heights and the two of them almost certainly mated just out of my sight. The peregrines were certainly going to breed in the nestbox!

Not the best of timing but I had long booked a very exciting birdwatching holiday for the crucial period 28th March to11th April. Yet I knew on my return that I would find that everything had gone 'as planned'. And so it had, as confirmed by detailed observations made by Chris Phillips which he kindly passed to me. I especially noted the following. On the morning of 2nd April Chris had seen the male in the nestbox with the female perched just to one side of it; when the male left the box, the two peregrines copulated and the male then flew off. Late in the afternoon Chris saw the female inside the box while the male was perched on a Chartwell Court balcony. After taking off and flying in high circles over Russell and Clarence Squares, thus probably displaying to the female, he landed by the box and when after a few minutes the female left it and flew to Chartwell Court, the male followed her, the two of them copulated, and once again the male flew off. That same day a building surveyor had checked the box to ensure it had been securely fixed and had been surprised to find a large mottled brown egg inside! On the morning of the 7th Chris saw the male arrive with a pigeon, pluck it on the top of Sussex Heights, then take off again carrying the plucked pigeon and transfer it in mid-air to the female who took her prepared meal to eat on a balcony floor of Chartwell Court. Chris wrote how pleased he was to see that the male was being both a dutiful partner and a thoughtful one to boot in not only supplying his mate with food but in pluck-ing it first. The following day, however, saw Chris's approval of the male's behaviour change somewhat. Not everything was going 'to plan'. The male arrived with a house martin, the first Chris had seen that year, and he fervently wished the peregrines would chase and catch only feral pigeons. This was a wish I would later very much share with him.

After my return on 11th April I was, of course, immensely pleased to learn the peregrines were incubat-ing eggs, three of them we would later learn, though one would fail to hatch. All watchers were impressed with the solicitous behaviour of the male, both in providing food for his mate and in doing his share of incubation. However, on 20th April I noticed that sometimes the eggs were definitely left unattended. When at about 5pm that afternoon I saw the male enter the nestbox, I was very surprised to see that the female did not leave it. As it turned out, she must have been already hunting because some time later she arrived with a catch, took it to the top of Sussex Heights and then disappeared with it below the parapet. Four days later John Reaney and I met in St Nicholas Cemetery which was our new vantage point for observing the peregrines. Very unusually, Sussex Heights was that afternoon shrouded in slowly clearing mist so we had to wait patiently for the mist to lift until at about 5pm we could once again see the nestbox. Fifteen minutes after that the male floated on to the parapet of Sussex Heights where he remained for only two minutes or so before he entered the nestbox; the female came out, flew to Chartwell Court, preened, went on two short flights to stretch her wings, and then she disappeared on to the floor of the favoured balcony of Chartwell Court, presumably to eat a meal from her larder, after which she flew to the parapet of Sussex Heights where she still was when John and I left at 6.40. This meant that the male had been incubating for over 80 minutes. At 6.15 before I left, I had seen my first swift of the year arriving, perilously so, high over Sussex Heights, but happily unmolested by the peregrines probably because one was incubating and the other was already dining!

The next big event, of course, would be the hatching of the eggs and during the first week of May I expectantly checked each day the behaviour of the two peregrines at the nestbox. However, it wasn't until 11th May that I noticed an extremely agitated male peregrine continually peering into the nestbox, then moving away but repeatedly returning to have another good look. The eggs were hatching! The female was in attendance but the progressive male peregrine just couldn't keep away! Perhaps he should have been already hunting for his new family but these were probably his very first chicks hatching and his curiosity was clearly overwhelming! That evening I phoned Peter Whitcomb with the good news and the following evening the peregrine falcons' best friend, Graham Roberts. Many people were excited at this dramatic turn of events, including occupants in Sussex Heights and in houses around Russell Square, especially, I remember, the owner of the Sandpiper Guest House, his wife and their daughter.

When the chicks were about twelve days old, Graham and his father, having duly obtained permission from English Nature, went on to the rooftop of Sussex Heights to inspect the chicks in their nestbox, two of them, and to remove an infertile egg for chemical analysis. It seemed very ironic to me that Graham Roberts of all people should have had to obtain permission from English Nature to approach the nestbox when English Nature had previously been unable to help protect the peregrines as, for that matter, had the regional RSPB. However, now the peregrines were breeding in Graham's nestbox, it was extremely desirable that both these prestigious and important bodies should be fully on board.

Another birdwatching holiday then intervened for me but on my return on 8th June I was delighted to see that the two large chicks, therefore both female, were very visible in the nestbox and, indeed, were beginning to venture on to the roof parapet. The morning of 13th June I spent in the cemetery with Peter Whitcomb keeping the two chicks and their parents under close observation. Much to our pleasure a hobby flashed across the sky above our heads, the only one I have ever seen in Brighton. The chicks were now spending an increasing amount of time on the roof, often flapping their wings, and it wouldn't be too long, I thought, before they would embark on their maiden flights, surely perilous undertakings in such a built-up area. But even before these maiden flights happened, there was a crisis.

On Sunday, 21st June, John Reaney phoned to say that only one chick was now visible and that therefore the other chick had somehow been 'lost'. I couldn't believe it. All through the week, I, John Reaney and Chris Phillips kept anxious watch on the parapet but, as John had told me, only one chick was visible and, moreover, this one surviving chick would surely soon launch herself into the void on that all-important and hazardous first flight. Would we 'lose' this second chick as well? However, when around lunchtime the following Sunday I suddenly saw as if by magic two chicks on the parapet I could scarcely believe my eyes. And after I'd rubbed them there were still two chicks on the parapet! As soon as possible I phoned John Reaney who later told me he had virtually run to the cemetery to confirm my sighting. Had I seen a mirage? No, I hadn't. The crisis of one lost peregrine chick was over. The missing chick had presumably spent a week behind and below the parapet and therefore hidden from view but somehow that Sunday morning she had successfully managed to flutter on to the parapet and rejoin her sister.

When one crisis ends, another begins. That afternoon was to be traumatic for all of us. A mere two hours after I'd seen the two chicks together again on the parapet, one of them launched herself off it as she had been threatening to do. It was that all-important maiden flight. She flew strongly but failed to regain the height she needed in order to make a safe return to the parapet and we watched in dismay as we saw her lose more height and obviously make a crash-landing on or near the ground somewhere in the vicinity of Sussex Heights. Immediately John, Chris and I went to look for her, taking, I suppose, five minutes or so to arrive and we then scoured every square yard of wherever we could but we saw no chick. Had we all made a big mistake in wanting the peregrines to breed in the middle of an urban environment? But the chick had been stupid! If only she had turned east and then south!, she would have found any number of balconies she could have safely landed on. She ought to have thought things out thoroughly before so precipitately launching herself! That evening I phoned the sad news to both Graham Roberts and Peter Whitcomb that once again we had 'lost' one of the two chicks.

It was at about 5pm next day that the remaining chick, undaunted, made her maiden flight, no doubt having been chivvied by concerned parents to do better than her sister. At any rate, both parents stayed in close flight attendance but seemed far more of a hindrance, I thought, than a help. Like her sister the day before, the chick tried to make the desired return to the parapet, failed by only a foot or so, slithered down the building's north face, tried to perch on one of the face's narrow window ledges, again failed, but, luckily or otherwise, turned east then south, and crash-landed in the middle of a garden balcony on the east face of Sussex Heights. Considerable damage had been done, I was sure, to the flowers of the balcony garden but it was all in an excellent cause. I never discovered if the flat's gardener ever found out who or what had so mysteriously 'disarranged' his or her flowers. For when I later returned to my lookout post I stared long and hard in both disbelief and delight at the sight of the chick with her parents once again on the parapet of Sussex Heights? How had she got there? I phoned the good news to Peter Whitcomb.

The next day, the last in June, there was still only one chick visible on the parapet so I feared that the first chick had undoubtedly come to an untimely end. But since the surviving chick could obviously negotiate a safe return to the parapet and therefore to the nestbox, I was no longer concerned for her safety. However, next day I saw that this chick had braved once more that looming void beyond the north face and I eventually spotted her on the floor of one of the balconies of Chartwell Court. Now my concern was whether she would be able to scramble from the floor to the balcony railing and so take off again. Of course, I knew that the parents would continue to feed her. But what about the occupants of the flat? I needn't have worried because the building's porters told me that the flat was temporarily unoccupied. Then came the wonderful news I had not been expecting to hear when John Reaney phoned to say there were now two chicks visible, one back on the parapet and one still in the Chartwell Court balcony. Just how many lives does a peregrine chick have? We later learned that a Good Samaritan taxi-driver had discovered the first chick in distress shortly after it had crash-landed, had managed to secure it and take it to a vet who had arranged for it to be restored to the parapet. It seemed that all Brighton and Hove was rooting for its marvellous peregrines.

But what of the second chick marooned in a Chartwell Court balcony? I had asked the building's porters if John and I could go to the balcony the following day to see if anything needed to be done. So, accompanied by one of the two helpful porters, John and I peered into a corner of the balcony to see a perfectly healthy-looking peregrine chick just a few feet away peering back at us. Properly concerned at the lonely isolation of this chick, the kindly children in the flat above had thrown down some toys for it to play with, including a rubber killer whale! John and I made a decision. If the chick was still on the balcony floor on the morrow, then we would return to the flat to give her a helping hand. That morning, to our happiness and relief, the chick was no longer on the Chartwell Court balcony floor but perched with her sister on the top of Sussex Heights with two proud parents in close attendance! The drama was over. From now on, I thought, it would be just a question of enjoying the antics of the two chicks as they frolicked with each other and with their parents and, above all, learned to hunt.

I was then unavoidably away until the middle of July when I was delighted to learn that the chicks had spread their wings sufficiently to include the West Pier in their daily sorties from the nestbox. Shortly after that, John Reaney presented to the extremely helpful porters of Chartwell Court a painting he had done of the peregrine chick peering at us from a corner of her temporary balcony home and to round off a memorable day we watched in the evening the male peregrine and one of his daughters, much bigger than her father, frolicking together at the West Pier. Although I never once saw at the West Pier the family of four peregrines together, John Reaney had this great pleasure towards the end of July. My greatest pleasure was to come one evening in early August when I saw the two chicks sky-dancing together for a full 20 minutes; 19/20 for performance, I decided, on the grounds that a strict former teacher like myself never gives full marks! Of course, dancing, diving and frolicking are all very well and no doubt essential but the chicks had to learn to kill and when on 15th August I saw one of them catch a pigeon at the West Pier I felt that the entire year was now complete and that it had been a great success, thanks almost entirely, of course, to Graham Roberts. It is certainly possible that the chicks remained in the area for another week or two but I do not remember making any more positive identifications. As far as I could tell, it was the two adult peregrines who remained in residence until the end of the year and, of course, beyond.

Although autumn had not yet officially arrived for me – I had not yet seen pied wagtails at the front – by the beginning of September I was once again making almost daily evening visits to the West Pier to check up on those marvellous peregrines. There is, after all, something reassuring about routine. However, at precisely 7.10pm on 8th September, something quite unexpected and quite extraordinary happened.

The Winter of 1998-99:
Ring-necked Parakeets Take to the Pier

I had been only a few minutes at the seafront, looking east-wards in the direction of the West Pier, when I heard a characteristic squawk-cum-yelp directly above me, looked up, and to my amazement saw a ring-necked parakeet disappear like a streak of lightning into the pier. I didn't think I had ever seen a bird fly quite so fast! My immediate thought was that even if a peregrine had been present at the pier, there was no way that parakeet would have become a peregrine dinner! But where had the parakeet come from and why on earth had it decided to roost in the pier? Would it be staying only one night or would it find the West Pier to its liking?

To my great satisfaction exactly the same happened the following evening. About half an hour before sunset I heard the unmistakeable call, looked up, and saw a parakeet dis-appear into the pier in what seemed the merest fraction of a second. So superlative seemed to me the parakeet's flying skills that I simply could not help but compare them to the apparently incomparable skills of the peregrine. Eventually a peregrine would surely have to show the parakeet who was the real master of the skies and, of course, the undis-puted owner of the West Pier, wouldn't it?

I could scarcely wait for the next sunset and, sure enough, when I heard the parakeet's call I looked up but this time, to my great pleasure, I saw not one but two para-keets streak side by side into the pier. The original parakeet had obviously felt able to recommend its new roosting site. I continued watching, hoping to see the sudden presence of a peregrine. However, some five minutes after the two parakeets had arrived, I saw one of them fly out of the pier and disappear over the hotels. It seemed the pier with its hundreds of feral pigeons and scores of thousands of starlings had not been to the liking of the undoubtedly more refined second parakeet. But when would the peregrines intervene?

Two evenings later I watched a parakeet fly into the pier and then after some twenty minutes I saw a peregrine settle on a balcony of Sussex Heights and another fly on to the pier. This was the first time I had seen parakeet and peregrines together. Would the parakeet prudently depart? I stayed until it was quite dark but saw no parakeet leave.

Three more evenings passed and each evening a single parakeet entered like lightning into the pier. This was to be in general how each winter evening passed. However, on the fourth evening two parakeets again entered the pier but this time both remained – or, rather, I saw no parakeet leave. Perhaps the pier's other inhabitants weren't so unacceptable after all.

Two more days went by and at last I saw what I'd been waiting for: a peregrine arrive before any parakeet and settle ominously on its hunting balcony on Sussex Heights. This was crunch time and I waited expectantly for a parakeet to appear. What would happen? A sparrowhawk left the pier and passed virtually under the nose of the falcon without provoking a reaction. Would it be different when the parakeet arrived? It was not. The peregrine just watched, very wisely so! There was no way at all, I thought, in which a peregrine could catch such a superlative flier as a parakeet. The falcon would simply be made to look an embarrassed also-flown.

Events next evening at the seafront were really very surprising. First, a lone parakeet passed by the Bedford Hotel but instead of entering the pier it veered northwards and disappeared. A few minutes later I was astonished to see three parakeets fly towards the pier, circle it and then disappear behind the hotels. Three parakeets! But they had not stayed. However, a minute later the three returned, circled the pier once more and then entered it. To my further surprise a fourth parakeet, which was probably the first one I had seen, appeared from the northwest and flew straight into the pier. Four parakeets! It wasn't long, though, before two of them very noisily left the pier to disappear westwards in the direction of Waterloo Street. What bizarre behaviour. I waited until it was quite dark before I decided to head in the direction of my equivalent to the West Pier.

Three more typical one-parakeet evenings went by but on the fourth evening two parakeets arrived, only for one to leave very soon afterwards. On the fifth evening three parakeets entered the pier, though one left immediately and five minutes later the other two left as well. Suddenly I noticed a possible reason. A pair of peregrines were perched on one of the pier's two diagonal 'lookout' wires. I continued to watch. The peregrines did nothing but half an hour later a fourth parakeet left the pier. I had seen three enter and four leave! The parakeet phenomenon was getting stranger and stranger. However, nothing unusual happened on my next visits though adding charm to the evenings were one or two wheatears on their way back to Africa, temporarily detained by the proximity of the sea.

A decisive evening was at the beginning of October when I arrived about an hour before sunset to observe, one by one, the arrival of three peregrines. One settled on the top of Cavendish House, one on the West Pier, and the third on the Metropole Hotel. If, I thought, a parakeet was ever to be pursued by peregrines, this was surely to be the evening. It seemed to me the three falcons were very strategically placed. If the parakeet came in, as it nearly always did, past Cavendish House, then it could be intercepted and pursued by the Cavendish House peregrine as it flew towards the apparent safety of the pier. But at that point the peregrine on the pier could take off to meet it and, if so, the hapless parakeet would presumably veer northwards to try to escape over the hotels. But its escape could then be cut off by the peregrine meeting it from the Metropole Hotel. Indeed, there would be no escape. It was all fiendishly clever! The parakeet duly came in past Cavendish House, called loudly as it nearly always did, and flew straight into the pier. Not a single peregrine moved a feather. Peregrines are very wise birds, they obviously know when they have more than met their match.

On 8th October a pied wagtail was at the seafront. Autumn – or, rather, winter – had therefore officially arrived.

There is very little more to say about the West Pier parakeets. Through October to January it was always exciting waiting to hear that characteristic call, look up

and invariably see a single parakeet, only very occasionally two, flying towards the pier. Sometimes I heard the
call but failed to see the parakeet. Even less frequently
I managed to see the parakeet without hearing a call at
all. I became a great admirer of these exotic parrots, so
much so that towards the end of January I made what
amounted to a pilgrimage to the poplar trees in the Esher
Rugby Ground (by Hersham railway station). Only after
about a thousand ring-necked parakeets had come to
roost did I stop counting. It was a fantastic, inspiring
sight. Indeed, it was difficult to believe I was not in the
middle of India, though the general environs at all times
looked reassuringly like England. However, very sadly,
just five days after my pilgrimage to that famous London
roost, the parakeets disappeared from the West Pier. On
2nd February, at exactly 4.35pm, two parakeets, watched
by a pair of peregrines, flew like streaks of lightning into
the pier and that was the last time I was ever to see parakeets at the pier or, for that matter, in Brighton and Hove
City. It had been a very strange but exciting, enchanting
interlude.

1999-2003: The Triumph of the Peregrines

With the disappearance of the parakeets, my attention
turned once more to the activities of the pair of peregrines
which, without doubt, were going to breed for a second
time in the Sussex Heights nestbox. Indeed, thanks to
Graham Roberts, the battle to secure a future for the West

Pier peregrines had been well and truly won. Not only were the local regional RSPB and English Nature now fully on board but local inhabitants both in and around Sussex Heights had become very protective of 'their' peregrines. Members of the Regency Square Area Society in particular had begun taking great care of their new neighbours. There was no longer any reason to suppose that a pair of peregrines would not successfully breed each year in their skyscraper nestbox. Any fledgling chick coming to grief would be quickly found, dusted down and returned to the parapet. All that remained for me was to pay an occasional visit to the cemetery lookout and from there to watch and enjoy the peregrine spectacular.

By 7th April four eggs had been laid in the nestbox (according to the SOS Annual Report for 1999) and although these eggs successfully hatched, a storm on 16th May resulted in the death of one of the chicks. Once again the adult peregrines had used as a cache-site an open balcony belonging to an absentee flat owner in Chartwell Court and on the day the three chicks launched themselves successfully from their skyscraper parapet, John Reaney and I went on the balcony to do a thorough cleaning before a very indignant flat owner could return to be properly horrified. An enormous mass of rotting carcasses and countless maggots greeted us. Apart from the many carcasses of starlings and feral pigeons, John remembers identifying those of a woodcock, bar-tailed godwit and black-necked grebe – all easy prey for a peregrine. It was with some satisfaction and relief that I noted there was nothing to suggest the remains of a ring-necked parakeet! Nevertheless, I fervently wished the peregrines would stick to catching starlings and feral pigeons and leave other birds alone.

By the middle of July both parents had taken their three daughters – once again no male chicks – to experience the delights of the West Pier and it wasn't long before I had the great pleasure of watching three large peregrine chicks playing together above and around their seaside second home. On the last day of the month I had to laugh as I watched the three chicks frolicking with their father, making him look almost diminutive in comparison. When, I asked myself, is this male peregrine going to sire a male offspring?

On the day immediately before this family frolicking, something very unusual and a bit alarming had happened. A swimmer treading water close to the pier with just his head bobbing above the waves had been dived on by one of the peregrines which had pulled out of its dive only a foot or two above the swimmer's head. One very fortunate swimmer continued to tread water, blissfully unaware that he had come very close to being scalped! What on earth had that peregrine been up to: an inspection out of curiosity or just fun and games? Surely that bobbing head hadn't looked like an inviting, floating duck!

After about the middle of August only the two adult peregrines remained at the West Pier accompanied by one to three sparrowhawks as daily visitors. Sadly, kestrels were now a very infrequent sight. Perhaps the most unusual visitor was a clouded yellow butterfly in the middle of August, the first but not the last time I would see this gorgeous yellow jewel gracing the Brighton and Hove seafront. Nothing more unusual happened until Christmas Day when I went to see the falcons but saw instead a Concorde flying gracefully past the pier. A beautiful shape, certainly, and regal in flight but nowhere approaching the majesty of design and flight performance of a peregrine falcon or ring-necked parakeet (with the exception, of course, of brute speed).

During the year 2000 everything again went well for the Sussex Heights peregrines. The first of three eggs was laid on 1st April and by the middle of May the chicks had hatched. About a week afterwards a most unexpected and thrilling event occurred (for the lucky witnesses). I arrived at the cemetery lookout in the late afternoon to be greeted by a "Did you see it?" from John Reaney and Chris Phillips in what must have been a rehearsed unison! "See what?" I asked innocently. "Then you didn't," they both replied in the same unison and rather gleefully I thought! John told me what had happened. Alerted by the cries of gulls, John and Chris had looked up to see no less than an osprey approaching from the east and passing between Sussex Heights and the cemetery where John and Chris were. Both peregrines had aggressively mobbed the unwelcome intruder, with the osprey half rolling on to its back and extending its talons whenever the falcons had got too close for the osprey's comfort. Even when the perceived threat to their chicks had disappeared to the west, both peregrines had apparently remained very agitated, making dashing flights over Sussex Heights and even after the female had returned to her chicks, the male had continued to display his agitation, repeatedly rising and diving around his skyscraper territory. How very remarkable! If I had looked up and seen an osprey flying west along and high over Western Road I would have immediately entered a Dollond and Aitchison for an eye-check!

The three chicks, which had been so assiduously protected by their parents, grew very quickly and as in the previous two years their size showed them to be female. This meant that the pair of Sussex Heights peregrines (as far as I knew, the same two peregrines) had raised eight female chicks and no males (disregarding one infertile egg and the chick which had died in a storm). According to my calculations, the probability of this happening was one chance in 256! No matter, the chicks were healthy and in the last week of June were flying strongly. A week or so into July I watched the three of them frolicking together around the top of Sussex Heights watched over by their mother and on 17th July I saw the complete family, the two parents and their three daughters perched together by the nestbox. Well done, Graham Roberts! The new millennium had started very auspiciously for the West Pier peregrines. And, yes, eventually a male chick was produced by the two peregrines! In 2001 three chicks hatched and when one died just a few days later it was fed to its two siblings, one of whom turned out to be that so elusive male which on 20th June I saw successfully flying around the top of Sussex Heights. Of course, it wasn't long before the parents had introduced their chicks to the pleasures of the West Pier, as in the previous three years. Is my peregrine story now complete? Not quite, the story has a final twist!

The twist begins with the observation that after conducting more than 25,000 people around the pier since the beginning of 1997, at the end of 2001 the West Pier Trust was obliged to cancel all future tours because the pier's structure was deemed to have become too dangerous. There was, of course, a silver lining to such a menacing cloud. From the peregrines' perspective, those pesky, intrusive humans were no longer setting foot in their beloved sanctuary! Good year, then, for a celebration, 2002!

But how to celebrate? For four consecutive years the pair of peregrines had bred successfully in the nestbox provided for them by Graham. But not in 2002! Because by then I had more or less left the peregrines to the care of the Regency Square Society and was unavoidably away from Brighton through most of mid-May to mid-June, I have to rely on comments made by the Regency Square Society about the peregrines' curious and anomalous behaviour during the 'celebratory' spring of 2002. For after seemingly preparing in mid-March to lay eggs in Graham's nestbox, the peregrines then vanished and did not appear again on Sussex Heights until 18th April, followed by appearances on 21st and 27th. How strange. Why had the peregrines rejected the nestbox after four successful years of using it? Untoward human disturbance on Sussex Heights? Nevertheless, they still managed to breed. Somewhere! After an absence of nearly two months both adults were once again seen on the skyscraper and on 24th June not only were the adults again on Sussex Heights but they were accompanied by a chick and "there were another two chicks on the West Pier amongst the cormorants." The Society concluded that the peregrines had presumably bred on the West Pier and they noted that all three chicks were once again female. At the end of June Peter Whitcomb phoned to say that five peregrines had been seen on the West Pier, the two parents and their three daughters.

Extraordinary! Did the peregrines really succeed in 2002 in breeding on the West Pier, now no longer subjected to human disturbance? And if not the West Pier, then where? Whatever the reasons they had for abandoning their Sussex Heights nestbox, if these wonderful birds did breed on the West Pier then they had taken their last chance to pay homage to the Grand Old Lady which had served peregrines so well ever since Dozy had blazed the trail in that glorious month of December 1993.

In the spring of 2003 the West Pier was tragically and criminally burnt down, leaving only a forlorn, empty, iron skeleton. Thankfully, by then the seemingly prescient peregrines had already safely returned to their Sussex Heights nestbox and that summer they successfully managed to fledge three chicks, all three of them male. Yes, all three of them!

Final Years at the West Pier Seafront, 2000-2003

Obviously the peregrines would now be less frequent visitors to the burnt-out skeleton of what had once provided them with a permanent base and had harboured for them an inexhaustible supply of feral pigeons. But, of course, thanks to Graham Roberts, they now had a permanent base and nest site on Sussex Heights and each subsequent spring they would make proper use of it. However, what of the

West Pier's wintering starlings. Would the burning down of the pier necessarily put an end to their sunset arrivals at their former roost? First there is a sorry national tale to tell. In 2002 the country's leading conservation organisations red-listed none other than the once numerous starling as a species of high conservation concern! It seemed unbelievable. How could the starling, the common starling, have possibly come to such an apparently critical state? Was not the starling, like the once ubiquitous house sparrow, an indestructible species able to survive, and survive easily, no matter what was thrown at it? Apparently not. And I have my own local sorry tale to tell. Every winter from 1993 to 2003 I had watched starlings roosting at the West Pier and every winter I had found to my concern that their number appeared considerably lower than that of the winter before. By 2003 it seemed to me that their wintering number had fallen to a catastrophic ten percent or so of their huge total only ten years earlier. And now, in that terrible spring of 2003, the starlings' winter roost had been totally burnt out, leaving those starlings returning for the winter of 2003-4 and all future winters with far fewer places to perch and all of them totally exposed at night to the sea's merciless elements. Would they of necessity desert their one-time roost and seek shelter elsewhere? Of course they would. They would have to. But they didn't! Perhaps a minority forsook the skeletal West Pier for its Palace-cum-Brighton sister but the magnificent majority stayed on. And each winter they still come in as of old, sometimes dancing around for up to an hour or so before going to roost on what must be the most unpleasant and inhospitable sleeping quarters in the entire UK. So my own sorry tale has, after all, an inspiring end. What magnificent birds are starlings!

But what of the hundreds of peregrine-pleasing feral pigeons that had made the derelict West Pier their permanent, all-year residence? These, of necessity, did desert the burnt-out pier. Permanent residence had to be found elsewhere. Now only a handful of pigeons fly in each sunset to spend an exposed night on that barren, unwelcoming iron skeleton. Surprisingly, with the disappearance of the pigeons, the skeletal West Pier seems to have lost its attractiveness to both hungry peregrines and sparrowhawks: live starlings are, apparently, not a sufficient enticement to attract these raptors, last-resort carrion being, of course, no longer available on the burnt-out pier. In any case, to a peregrine a starling can only be, at best, a welcome snack whereas a pigeon is a proper meal! But where are the sparrowhawks? On my admittedly very infrequent visits to the post-2003 West Pier I have yet to see a visiting sparrowhawk, though, of course, there may be the occasional one or two or even more. I do hope so. After all, prior to 2003 both peregrines and sparrowhawks were by no means averse to catching starlings. Perhaps this winter of 2007-8 I shall once again visit every sunset and find out once again what is really going on at the West Pier seafront.

Apart from those always eye-catching peregrines, magnificent starlings and juicy, hunger-satisfying feral pigeons, what were some of the other birding and wildlife attractions I noticed during my last years of regular watching at the seafront? There were many attractions. On the first day of October 2000 I was astonished to see a red admiral and two clouded yellow butterflies seemingly determined to return over the sea to mainland Europe from whence, presumably, they had come. I feared they would not be successful.

Early in 2001 I met at the seafront a fellow peregrine watcher, Chris Walker, who told me that on his way to the front the previous summer he had passed through Regency Square and had been surprised to see a black redstart gathering insects and flying over rooftops in the direction of Western Road. A pair had obviously been attempting to breed. It wasn't difficult to locate the probable nest site but unfortunately from the redstarts' viewpoint I found this once rather derelict site was undergoing restoration. Black redstarts are very partial to a bit of rubble! Had they tried to breed in previous summers? After all, in early April 1996 I had seen a black redstart loitering by the boating pool almost opposite Regency Square.

At the end of February I watched about 500 brent geese fly eastwards past the West Pier and seven days into March a colourful party of some 20 oystercatchers did the same. In the first days of 2002 I was able to admire scores of gannets not too far out to sea and one day I even deserted the West Pier for its Palace sister in order to get much closer to these truly spectacular birds. My last sighting of note before I more or less abandoned birdwatching at the seafront was at the end of April 2003 of a dark-phase arctic skua very close to the shore and showing so well its long, pointed, central tail feathers which I think are such an attractive feature of this skua.

Why did I gradually abandon regular birdwatching at the West Pier seafront? It wasn't only because of the increasing attraction of St Ann's Well Gardens but the sea-front itself had become increasingly and depressingly less attractive to me – and to birds. When I first began frequent visits in December 1993, the front was a paradise for bird-watchers and for birds: it was a wild, such a wild place especially in winter. I and others often stood nearby or in front of the derelict Milkmaid Pavilion watching from there the West Pier and, alongside and behind us, the seafront and the roadside hotels. The roof of the Milkmaid Pavilion was grass strewn and particularly beloved by grey wagtails who would seek refuge there if disturbed from their boating pool winter sanctuary with its collection of irresistible puddles. To the west of the pavilion there was a series of lawns, bushes, vegetation and rockeries much appreciated by resident birds such as house sparrows, blackbirds, wrens and dunnocks and to spring and autumn passage migrants such as wheatears.

Alas, by April 1996 the Pavilion had been transformed into the architecturally elegant and excellent Italian restaurant, Alfresco, and by the end of the year the boating pool and its surrounding rockery had been transformed by the city council into a petanque court, for good measure the living earth between the 'rocks' of concrete replaced with life-less cement. The council's Seafront Development Initiative was well and truly underway but to a birdwatcher it might more appropriately have been called the Bird Habitat Disappearance Initiative. All the lawns and vegetation between the Alfresco restaurant and the so-called Peace Statue at the beginning of the Hove lawns were systematically replaced by bird-unfriendly habitats. Immediately to the west of Alfresco's a children's playground was created – a really attractive playground and certainly much used by parents and children except perhaps in winter months – but further to the west the council created just a long concrete desert ending in yet another arid petanque court. The large colony of nationally declining house sparrows was, at best, displaced as this part of the seafront was transformed almost literally from green to grey.

And then came the last tragic days of the beloved and magnificent West Pier. On 29th December 2002 during severely inclement winter weather, a part of the concert hall nearly collapsed into the sea and with it a section of the walkway between it and the pier head. Three weeks later, battered by a high tide of pounding waves and a relentless southerly gale, the already endangered concert hall suffered a further collapse. Yet the West Pier was hanging on, the pier head still defiantly intact. But what the ferocity of the elements couldn't accomplish, human criminality could. That spring the West Pier was completely burnt down, the pier head on 28th March, the concert hall on 11th May, two infamous days which marked so sad an end to my devotion to the glorious, derelict West Pier and to its once green, abandoned seafront. Happily, by this time I was already frequently visiting another excellent birdwatching habitat, very different indeed from the once wild, so wild West Pier seafront. This new irresistible attraction was the very sedate and respectable city park having the attractive name of St Ann's Well Gardens.

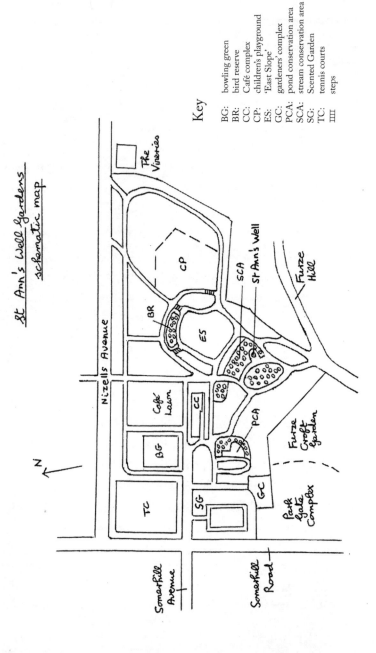

St Ann's Well Gardens
schematic map

N

Somerhill Avenue

Somerhill Road

Nizells Avenue

The Vineries

Furze Hill

Furze Croft Garden

Park Gate Complex

Café Lawn

St Ann's Well

Key

BG: bowling green
BR: bird reserve
CC: Café complex
CP: children's playground
ES: 'East Slope'
GC: gardeners' complex
PCA: pond conservation area
SCA: stream conservation area
SG: Scented Garden
TC: tennis courts
IIII: steps

Chapter Two

Hove's Avian Oasis: St Ann's Well Gardens

Just how did the park come to get its attractive name? It appears that in Saxon days of yore there lived in a large castle by the little village known as Brighthelm the beautiful maiden Lady Annefrida, happily betrothed since her childhood to Wolnoth, son of the Thane of Hollingbury. While anxiously awaiting the return from the wars of her true love and thence their immediate marriage, Lady Annefrida was to receive the terrible news that Wolnoth had been vilely ambushed and cruelly slain – it transpired by a wicked rival for her love – and that his lifeless body lay nearby on Gorse (Furze) Hill. Inconsolable and grief stricken by her loss, Lady Annefrida shed so many tears each day over the spot where her betrothed had been slain that the faithful Wolnoth returned to her in a dream to promise his true love that her tears would not be in vain "for where they fell, a Healing Spring Shall Rise And Flow For Evermore". And, verily, a healing spring did rise with the result that the pious maiden, who, alas, died but three years later, became known as Saint Ann and her spring of tears as St Ann's Well. Many years passed but the story did not die. By the end of the 19th century the entire woodland site had become known as St Ann's Well and Wild Garden or, more briefly, as St Ann's Well Gardens. In 1882 the *Brighton Gazette* patriotically described St Ann's miraculous spring as one of the finest in Europe, noting, quite properly, that it was "pleasantly shaded in summer by trees, and rendered additionally delightful by the carolling of birds".

The entire private site comprising some 12 acres of natural woodland was sold in 1907 to Hove Council by a Mr d'Avigdor Goldsmid for the bargain price of £10,000 freehold and officially opened to the public by the Mayor of Hove on 23rd May 1908. Since the owner was offered considerably more than twice that price by developers, the good people of Hove certainly owe a huge debt of gratitude to Mr Goldsmid for his generosity and commendable public spirit. Sad to say, however, despite its miraculous origin, the healing spring failed to flow for evermore but more or less dried up in the 1930s because of the construction of artesian wells nearby. In 1935 the pump house for the spring was demolished and the well covered over. However, a decorative well was eventually built to mark the site of the spring's pump house and where an informative plaque now reminds visitors to the well of the tragic origin of the park's attractive name.

But not just an attractive name, it is a most attractive park. First and foremost perhaps, despite the ravages of that Great October Storm of 1987, some 200 mature trees still remain from that original woodland. Of the many species in the park there are oak, evergreen oak, elm, sycamore, plane, maple, horse chestnut, sweet chestnut, hornbeam, ash, willow, poplar, beech, lime, silver birch, alder, tulip trees and others. The gardens are often a visual feast. Each spring a glorious display of crocuses and daffodils forms a stunning array of white, mauve and yellow colours while from the main entrance along Somerhill Road visitors are treated to an almost indescribably beautiful walkway between two lines of cherry trees in pink blossom. Apart from the park's many flower beds to delight the eye, there are also tennis courts for the fit and agile, a bowling green for the perhaps not quite so fit and agile, and for those starting out in life an extensive children's playground. And after all that exertion, the highly praised Garden Café offers ice-creams, tea and coffee, and delicious meals. Then there is the park's pond which always contains an impressive variety of conspicuous fish much to the happiness and enthusiasm of the pond's many young visitors and their parents. But not only humans are attracted to the pond. With its water continually circulated and filtered through gravel and watercress and flanked by four substantial clumps of bamboo and other vegetation, the pond abounds in summer damselflies and other insects while throughout the year many kinds of birds come not only to quench any thirst but for a bathe in the pond's perpetual waterfall. And this brings me to why I now regard St Ann's Well Gardens as my second home, certainly my 'patch', which is its surprising variety of breeding and wintering birds and short-stay avian visitors on migration from and back to Africa.

Living so close, I myself had quite often visited St Ann's Well Gardens without ever spending a lot of time there. I had other things to do. Nevertheless, in the autumn of 1999 I began to visit quite frequently and was very pleased to encounter a grey wagtail regularly enjoying the delights of the pond's irresistible waterfall, supported by a seductive cast of foraging goldcrests and elusive treecreepers, one of my favourite birds. However, what excited me most was the frequent presence of a family party of some eight long-tailed tits, active as always, continually dashing through the trees, seemingly never spending long enough to down a substantial meal. Such a winter family party meant the possibility of springtime breeding and as I looked around I realised that several nesting sites were available. As a boy I had never seen long-tailed tits, much though I had searched for them, because the ferocious winter of 1947 had virtually eliminated these frail little birds from the northeast Norfolk coast where I was born and grew up. But here in St Ann's Well Gardens perhaps I had breeding long-tailed tits just about on my doorstep! I longed for the spring to arrive. When it did, it was to be for me the beginning of an emotional rollercoaster and an ongoing love affair with St Ann's Well Gardens as I began to appreciate more and more its wealth of birdlife. This love affair is still very much on-going but in this little book – it has to have an end! – I choose to cut off my affectionate observations of the park's long-tailed tits and, indeed, of all its many other birds and wildlife by the late autumn of 2007, some 20 years, there-fore, after that Great October Storm of 1987 paid its so cruel visit to this magnificent park.

The Saga of the Long-tailed Tits, 2000-2007

Year 2000

It wasn't until early April that I revisited the long-tailed tits and was delighted to find a pair much in evidence in the vicinity of two parallel lines of thick, welcoming, prickly berberis bushes. This was surely the tits' chosen nest site. The park seemed alive with resident birds and everywhere I looked I saw song thrushes, such a welcome sight since the song thrush was in serious national decline. I felt like writing to the council to express my appreciation of its staff's sympathetic, knowledgeable maintenance of the park, a haven both for people and wildlife. My anxious wait for the tits to begin feeding young ended on 23rd April, although I still couldn't pinpoint, even using binoculars, the extremely well-hidden nest deep in the berberis. To my pleasure I realised I wasn't the only person interested in the tits (though perhaps the only one who knew what they were called!). Many people admired and commented on the beauty of these little jewels which seemed to do everything possible to attract attention, especially by regularly hovering for a few seconds directly over their nest site before assiduously attending to the needs of obviously ravenous youngsters.

On the morning of 8th May the youngsters fledged and I counted at least five in a nearby tree. There was no reason, I thought, why long-tailed tits should not breed successfully every year in such a tailor-made site. However, later that day the head gardener told me the rather devastating news that the line of berberis favoured by the tits was soon to be removed in order to make way for water plants to be grown alongside a renovated stream which was to run from near the park's ornamental well, pass under a principal path and after some 30 yards disappear into the ground at the far end of the berberis bushes. It seemed to me very doubtful that the tits would attempt to breed in the remaining line of berberis if only because to the tits the then isolated berberis would appear to provide insufficient protection from intruders, human or otherwise.

A few days later I wrote to the council official then responsible for overseeing the maintenance of the park and whose idea it was to create the new stream and water plant habitat. I expressed heartfelt appreciation for the existence of this attractive park virtually in the centre of Brighton and Hove, explained my concern for the future of what I considered to be the jewel in the park's avian crown, namely the long-tailed tits, and suggested a few improvements for providing even better habitats for the park's wildlife. There was an immediate response from this official and when we later met in the gardens it was with much pleasure that I realised the official was sympathetic both to my idea of planting a second line of berberis on the non-stream side of the remaining line of berberis and to the possibility of turning a bare patch of hard soil into a bird reserve by enclosing it with a fence and planting the area with vegetation, especially brambles, to try to encourage spring passage warblers to stay to breed. If finances were available both my suggestions would be acted on.

In the middle of May the juvenile long-tailed tits reminded me of their presence when I watched them moving nimbly away every time a marauding crow seemed to have got within striking distance. These masked little elves really did appear quite unconcerned by the crow's persistence. Sadly, at the beginning of August the line of berberis which had been a home to the tits through April and May was removed but six weeks later a compensatory line of berberis was planted as I had suggested. Unfortunately, several of the planted bushes didn't take so that new bushes had eventually to be planted and at present the second line of planted berberis still remains totally inadequate from a tit-nesting perspective. Indeed, no long-tailed tits have since successfully bred in any of the remaining berberis bushes. On a more positive note, the juvenile tits that had fledged in the spring evidently managed to evade all would-be predators and every now and then I would see a large family party scampering around the park until well into December and, indeed, beyond into January.

Year 2001

The last time in winter I saw this family party of long-tailed tits was on 24th January when, to my surprise, two of them left the main group and began to prospect for a nest site in a clump of berberis adjacent to the park's pond. This was very clearly what the two were doing! Moreover, to my even greater surprise, the two of them began nest building just four days later, a very early date it seemed to me. Their commitment to defending their pond nest became apparent when, in the middle of February, yet again to my surprise, I saw how agitated both tits became when a male house sparrow visited their nest berberis. I was to discover the reason for such agitation three years later but that February I asked myself what possible threat could an inquisitive house sparrow pose to a long-tailed tits' nesting site.

A few days later Peter Whitcomb visited the park and immediately on entering via Nizells Avenue, heard and saw two long-tailed tits in a tree by a main path adjacent to a large berberis bush. Perhaps there was more than one pair in the park!

In the meantime two small boys had decided to build a hideout directly under the tits' nest in the pond berberis (in a forbidden area but boys being boys…). Nevertheless, amazingly so, the tits continued building even with the boys' heads often just two feet or so below their nest. These tits were not only brave but impressively persistent nest builders. The first five days and nights of March were bitterly cold, yet instead of only feeding during the day to ensure warmth at night, both tits spent a lot of each daytime adding material to their nest. There clearly must have been an abundance of food for them to be able to spend so much time nest-building, a joint activity which, curiously, the two had now been engaged in for some six long weeks. An amusing event happened in early March. I saw a tit approach the nest site with a piece of white material which didn't look like a feather and then leave the nest after a minute or two and fly off. Immediately its partner entered the nest, flew out with the white material, took it outside the conservation area and discarded it. Carefully watching it float slowly to the ground, I went to examine it and discovered a piece of white paper! No wonder the nest building was taking so long!

In the middle of March I checked on the pair of tits along Nizells Avenue and saw they had started building a nest in the berberis bush near to where Peter Whitcomb had first seen them. This path nest (as I shall call it) was clearly only a few days old. By 3rd April it was finished, the construction completed therefore in about three weeks, though the pond nest, begun much earlier on 28th January, was still being built. How extraordinary! Even on 9th April I saw the pond tits still at work, this time carefully inserting a feather into their nest. A week later, while watching at the path nest, I saw the two long-tailed tits with two accompanying blue tits mob a very disgruntled male blackbird which had ventured too near to the path berberis and which then eventually retaliated by charging the aggressive tits several times before flying off. As I later worked out, whereas the quick-construction path tits were still about a week away from laying their first egg, the first egg laid by the slow-construction pond tits was some six days earlier on about 17th April. Nevertheless, this did not prevent one of the pond tits on 22nd April from inserting a further feather into their nest although the female had already laid between five to six eggs. It was all very strange. The only thing I knew for sure was that the pond tits were heroic in their apparent disregard of the activities of the two pesky boys immediately below their nest.

On 10th May the pond eggs hatched and I watched the nestlings being regularly fed, presumably just by the male since he was sporting his long, straight tail. But don't all long-tailed tits have a long, straight tail? Not always! Because when the female (the sole incubator) appeared the following day to feed her nestlings, I enjoyed a good laugh when I saw the end of her tail was quite curved! She had clearly failed to ensure that that long encumbrance always protruded through the nest hole entrance! On 27th May these pond nestlings fledged and I counted at least eight of them, side by side high up on the branch of an oak tree, some facing one way, some the other. It was a heart-warming sight. In cold and drizzle the path nestlings fledged on 2nd June and when I encountered two of them that day (total number unknown), they quite understandably seemed rather disconsolate!

In the meantime the area of bare, hard ground I had written about to the council had been fenced in and black-thorn planted alongside the fence. The future bird haven was well and truly underway and a year later was kindly planted with brambles by Chris Perry and a colleague from the Brighton Conservation Volunteers, watched over approvingly by an official from the council.

Although perhaps up to 20 long-tailed tits must have been in the vicinity during the summer of 2001, it was in late August when I next saw at least ten of these little gems dashing around the trees of a private garden close to the park. Thereafter I frequently came across a family party, once in early December accompanied by a treecreeper, and the year ended with the tits generously giving me a prolonged sighting. Would the New Year, I wondered, be just as engaging?

Year 2002

It was. But it was also disturbing. The pond tits began building on the early side as before, on about 9th February, but this time they had forsaken the berberis clump directly over the two boys' hideout and were building instead in a berberis hedge the other side of the clump just a few inches from a busy public path and a few feet from a much-used park bench. I was appalled. What were the two tits thinking of? They built slowly as during the year before but finished a little earlier on about 25th March. Two weeks before this, one of the tits had given me a laugh when I saw it struggling to the nest site bearing a white feather as long as the tit itself, including its tail! Egg-laying began on about 5th April and incubation about a week later. Every time I passed the hedge and gave a surreptitious glance towards the nest I would smile to myself on seeing a tail protruding from the nest hole: there would be no curved end of a tail this year! On 29th April the eggs hatched and the two adults then made sure that all those humans sitting on the adjacent park bench would watch them admiringly as they performed their crazy hovering directly over their nest site. Here in St Ann's Well Gardens it seemed that long-tailed tits and people co-existed admirably. Nevertheless, it was difficult to believe that the nest and its youngsters would not come horribly to grief during the 15 days or so of feeding. However, at 9.30 am on 13th May I arrived at the nest to see one cocky, very self-assured juvenile perched by its deserted home, seemingly without a care in the world, busily preening itself, before it then joined the other fledged youngsters deeper in the berberis hedge. I counted at least seven and concluded that the pond tits certainly knew what they were about.

But what about the path tits? Did they know what they were about? On 8th March I discovered their nest or,

93

rather, I discovered their two nests! They were both being built in an extensive hebe bush close to the very busy path running parallel to Nizells Avenue. Amazingly, at least to me, one nest was only about six inches above the other and displaced to one side by only a few inches. Each nest was already about two inches deep. I watched the pair of tits at work first on the lower nest and then on the higher. I watched unbelieving but, of course, could not watch for too long. The two tits obviously couldn't decide which nest they were supposed to be building and so they were building both! The confusion had presumably been caused by the two nest sites being virtually identical and located by the side of the same slightly sloping branch. Moreover, the two nests were very exposed and the immediate environs of the hebe bush were a favourite play area for small children. I gave the tits a very low probability of success.

One morning I walked past the very vulnerable hebe bush and saw both tits building at the lower nest but half an hour later both were building at the upper nest. What a lot of needless work the tits were engaged in. Interestingly, I never saw one tit building at one nest at the same time as its partner was building at the other: when together, they were always working on the same nest. By 19th March each nest was about half finished and therefore the two quick-fire tits had effectively built a complete nest in very fast time! Only they were very stupid long-tailed tits!

From then on, however, the path tits totally ignored the lower nest and four days later, on 23rd March, the upper nest was two-thirds finished. As I expected, it apparently never occurred to the tits to make use of material from their abandoned lower nest. On 1st April I saw the tits add a final feather to their now finished upper nest and a month later, on 2nd May, both parents were hard at work feeding ravenous youngsters. There were no major scares during this feeding period except in early May when very strong winds damaged the top of the nest and when I helped the pair of tits drive away a crow inspecting the hebe bush. By noon on 18th May the youngsters had fledged and on arriving I saw two fledglings in nearby bushes. Presumably there were others and it was surprising I saw no more juveniles in the park that summer or autumn. I hoped very much that the torrential rain after the pond tits had fledged had not caused any or at least many casualties. But the path tits had fledged in reasonably good weather.

It was with some relief when in early December I saw my first long-tailed tits of the winter, clearly nest prospecting in the same pond berberis hedge a pair had used in the spring. Unfortunately, a gardener subsequently removed the berberis bush next to the one the tits had used and this undoubtedly discouraged any building in the same hedge the following spring. However, I had remained optimistic, especially after seeing a family party foraging in the pond area in mid-December. Nevertheless, the year 2003 went by without my seeing any breeding long-tailed tits, either in the pond area or by the path alongside Nizells Avenue. Happily, the next year would be very different.

Year 2004

This leap year certainly started spectacularly when after a telephone call from Peter Whitcomb I took a train to Lewes to try to see the simply delightful white-headed long-tailed tits that had somehow managed to find their way to this Sussex metropolis from somewhere in eastern Europe. In the autumn of 2002 a week's birding extravaganza I had enjoyed in Hungary had nevertheless failed to give me even a glimpse of this white-headed race of long-tailed tits, certainly a major disappointment. And suddenly here they were, in Lewes! Thanks to the help of a sharp-eared birder, it wasn't long before I was watching three to four of these heart-warming, white-headed little charmers foraging in the company of a dozen or so of our own charming variety. It was a sight to behold and I returned to Brighton extremely grateful to Peter for passing on to me such vital information. I hardly ever twitch but I very definitely twitched on the 2nd February 2004!

Thus stimulated I sought out the long-tailed tits in St Ann's Well Gardens and was pleased to see both pond and path pairs begin building on the same day, 24th February. The pond tits had once again chosen to build in the same berberis hedge as in 2002 but this time further away from the bench and therefore reasonably distant from the gap so needlessly created the winter before. Moreover, the nest site was several inches inside the berberis hedge and to this extent adequately protected by its thorns. On the other hand, the path nest was rather exposed at the top of the same berberis bush used by the pair of 2001 and was very far from adequately protected. Once again I noted how after bitterly cold winter nights such as those of 26-28th February both pairs of tits continued building as if they had spent short balmy summer nights sleeping on well-supplied stomachs. By 9th March I saw that the exterior of the pond nest was finished but the exposed and more vulnerable path nest still lacked its top third.

That same morning I noticed a male house sparrow approach the path nest with the obvious intention, so I thought, of stealing nest material. To my great surprise, however, he simply deposited himself inside the nest with just his head protruding upwards from one side and his tail from the other. Very much at home he seemed too! When the two owners showed up, one carrying a feather, their consternation was immediate and dramatic. The feather was dropped and both tits jumped hither and thither around and about the nest until finally one of them gave the sparrow's head a glancing, in-flight blow with its bill which it followed with a tweak of the offender's protruding tail. This double assault proved enough to put the squatter to flight whereupon the tits immediately set about making repairs to their nest's damaged perimeter. But the sparrow was evidently no quitter for some ten minutes later he returned and once more took up illicit residence, thereby provoking the tits into a furious reaction which gave the squatter no peace at all. As if seeking a showdown, the would-be usurper eventually left the nest to perch defiantly a few inches above it, apparently challenging its lightweight owners to risk a direct attack. The latter, however, waited until the intruder had returned to their nest, then made life so uncomfortable for it that after a few more minutes the sparrow had seemingly had enough and flew off, leaving once again the rightful owners to reclaim their now somewhat larger nest. I never did think of a satisfactory explanation as to what that male house sparrow was up to!

Next morning I returned to find the tits building fever-ishly and also flying straight towards and so dislodging any sparrow which so much as happened to alight anywhere in their nest bush. With obvious constructional difficulties to be overcome in securing the dome, the nest's exterior was not successfully completed until about 25th March. A week later the path tits could still be seen around their abused, misshapen nest at about the time the pond tits began laying but thereafter they abandoned the nest completely. On 2nd April I noted to my surprise three tits by the pond nest but shortly afterwards one was driven off. However, three days later, on seeing four tits perched amicably together by the pond nest, I realised that the path tits must have deserted their nest in favour of joining forces with their two fellow tits at the more concealed pond nest some 150 yards away. I went to investigate possible reasons for this desertion and found a blackbird building in the berberis only a foot or so from the path tits' abandoned nest. This, presumably, must have been the last straw for the two plucky tits and on 13th April I saw that the blackbirds were incubating eggs in their unwelcome nest.

At the pond nest everything went well and nearly every time I walked past the nest I could see a tail protruding from the entrance hole. On 23rd April the eggs hatched but for six days afterwards I could still regularly see a pro-truding tail. The lucky nestlings were fed continually by, I assumed, four adults and there was much crazy hovering over the nest site, once for as long as about 20 seconds! Only once did I see a skirmish at the nest site between two adults but then they perched amicably together. On

10th May I had a charming sight of the four carers perched side by side on railings near to the nest, presumably taking a much needed break. Two mornings later I carefully watched from a distance the youngsters fledging, attended by their carers, but in the early evening there was no sign of the fledglings and to my alarm I saw their four carers near the nest site mobbing a magpie with something large in its bill. However, the following afternoon I watched about a dozen long-tailed tits flying between trees, most of them juveniles and therefore completely mobile. And the very next day I watched enchanted as the four adults and at least nine youngsters foraged together amidst the pink blossom of an ornamental cherry tree. A beautiful and inspiring sight. All's well that ends well.

But at least nine youngsters! Something troubled me. I returned to the nest and estimated that even with the nest being elastic no more that four youngsters, well, perhaps five at a terrible pinch, could have been squeezed into its ultimate expanded size. But at least nine! And if it is true that the adults also roost in the nest with their nestlings, then that meant between 11 to 13 tits in a nest with an absolute maximum capacity of five! Despite the fact that juveniles lack adult long tails, it is obvious that in their final pre-fledging period the juvenile long-tailed tits can only be packed and preserved in their nests by continuous divine intervention! Through June to September the tits seemed to disappear from the park but after the middle of October I periodically came across a feeding party of at least seven. The year had, in the end, been a successful one for the park's persistent and courageous long-tailed tits.

Year 2005

This year a pair of great spotted woodpeckers took up residence in the park and I spent much time trying to watch their every move. Nevertheless, I didn't entirely abandon the park's long-tailed tits and I was pleased to see that on 8th February the path pair had begun building, though in the same berberis which had not served them well the year before. Indeed, these two tits were probably the same ones as the previous year because they were extremely aggressive towards avian visitors and on 24th February I watched the pair combine to put to flight a male greenfinch and the following day a blue tit had to leave in a hurry! As before, no matter how cold the days and nights the tits still built: the penultimate day of February was bitterly cold with snow still falling but the tits built on. Their nest appeared finished on about 10th March but then, for reasons unknown, the tits abandoned it. This time, however, there was no nesting pair at the pond for them to join as an extended family endeavour.

To my surprise, on 12th March, a pair of long-tailed tits began building in the remaining line of mature berberis alongside the stream and I assumed that it was the path pair at work on a new nest. But perhaps it was the pond pair which had chosen a new nest site. At any rate, this pair built steadily and 16 days later the nest appeared all but finished. However, again for reasons unknown, perhaps because a gardener had been working by the stream, the tits abandoned this nest. Because I was spending so much time watching the pair of woodpeckers in the gardens I had lost track of what the park's long-tailed tits were up to.

Nevertheless, on 4th May I saw a pair of long-tailed tits around the path hebe bush and I guessed that perhaps the pair had a nest there. Then, a few days later, I saw a long-tailed tit at the pond with a curved tail, therefore it was clear that a female was incubating or had just finished incubating. Some two weeks after that, I saw a pair of tits feeding young in a nest in the path hebe bush – my guess had been correct – and on the last day of May I watched the parents hovering side by side over their nest. Was this to encourage those greedy yellow gapes at the nest hole to venture forth? At any rate, next day they had indeed ventured forth but I was not to see long-tailed tits again until the middle of September when a party of at least eight were foraging in the vicinity of the pond. Thereafter I frequently encountered a feeding party of these pugnacious little birds, often, of course, in the company of other tits and, charmingly so, of a wintering treecreeper. In November I watched the treecreeper find a food-filled crevice only for it to be driven off by one of the long-tailed tits. There may have been safety in numbers for the treecreeper but it's a bit much when your best finds get immediately taken over!

Year 2006

The year started promisingly with a pair of tits inspecting the berberis clump by the pond and by the end of January they were once again building. Slowly as usual but they continued during a period when the nights were bitterly cold and ice covered the pond during the day. I had noticed that through February there were often four tits together at the pond at dusk so I assumed that two pairs were roosting together for warmth. This probably meant that another pair were building in the park and on 1st March I discovered their nest in the path hebe bush. Unfortunately, it was very exposed at the top of this non-prickly site and through my binoculars it was easy for me to watch the tits completing the entrance hole from inside the nest. When I returned at the end of March from a two-week holiday I saw that the tits were still building, now adding feathers to the nest's lining. On 9th April I watched a tit enter the nest – therefore all was well – but two days later I found the too exposed nest had been predated, very probably by one of the park's many crows or magpies. After that disaster the pair of tits almost certainly decided to abandon the park, probably to try breeding in a private garden nearby. The pond tits did precisely this.

Everything had seemed to be going well for the pond tits but early in March the gardeners cut and lowered by up to two feet the berberis hedge close to the clump where the tits were building, so effectively ruling out the hedge as a nest site in the future. It was a great pity since the tits had twice successfully used the hedge and, moreover, to the obvious enjoyment of people watching their comings and goings from the adjacent park bench. However, the tits continued to build in the berberis clump and once I saw the two of them arrive together each carrying a feather. A day later the tits were extremely agitated by the frequent presence of a pair of house sparrows in and around their nest site and although one tit continued building, the other continually shadowed the sparrows, especially the male, wherever they and he went. When I returned from my holiday, there was no sign of breeding activity and I assumed the tits had forsaken the pond berberis for what they considered to be a safer site in a private garden nearby. This turned out to be the case for in the summer a very pleased resident of the Park Gate complex, a Mr Denis Cannan, showed me where a pair of long-tailed tits had successfully raised a large family in the Park Gate private garden running alongside the park and not far from the pond.

In the middle of June I encountered a family party of at least eight long-tailed tits frolicking by the pond and noticed with surprise one juvenile sporting an extremely long tail. Bizarrely, I saw two apparent copulations with an adult on top and a juvenile underneath. What was going on? Some two weeks later I watched two juveniles bathing in the waterfall and again saw what extremely long tails they had, longer, it seemed, than even normal adult length. Happily, I continued to see this family party, so it was reasonably clear the pond tits had indeed bred successfully and I hoped that the path tits had enjoyed success as well. Certainly through the months of September to December I kept encountering parties of long-tailed tits and I optimistically assumed that there were two family parties enjoying the hospitality of St Ann's Well Gardens.

Year 2007

Each year the pond and path long-tailed tits had continued to surprise me and 2007 was to be no exception. On 10th February I saw the pond pair of tits inspecting the clump of bamboo immediately to the left of the pond's principal entrance gate. Bamboo?! Since the pair seemed determined not to desert the pond as they had done the year before and since the pond's berberis was no longer serviceable, they were clearly turning their attention to the pond's clumps of bamboo. Bamboo?! For the rest of the month I saw them constantly entering the bamboo but not with nest material that I could see. However, on 2nd March I could see them taking in nest material and four days later I was at last able to make out the foundations of their nest at the top of the clump. That evening I wrote in my diary in block capitals, MADNESS! There was no way, I thought, that the tits could build their nest to withstand buffeting from severe wind, not to mention the continual presence of people passing alongside the bamboo on their way to the pond and clanging the metal gate behind them. Was I to be proved wrong? On 9th March the bamboo was being blown about violently in near gale-force winds but the tits went on building. More severe buffeting occurred on 18th but the tits had somehow firmly secured their nest to the stalks of bamboo. Next day Peter Whitcomb accompanied me to the pond and although he took photos of the bamboo he couldn't make the nest appear on them. Had he done so he would have all but achieved the impossible! On 21st the tits were still adding to their now perhaps half-finished nest but that was to be the last day I was to see them. I think what finally dissuaded the tits was the double raiding of the bamboo clump by a gang of little boys who thought that bamboo stalks made excellent substitutes for fencing rapiers! Their raids had made the nest become visible!

I was later told by Mr Cannan of the Park Gate complex that once again the tits had bred successfully in the private garden which meant that the pair had followed the same pattern as the year before. And sure enough, just like the year before, a family party of tits began to visit the pond from the second week of June onwards, with, curiously, at least two of the juveniles once again sporting exceptionally long tails.

Happily, the path tits which each year attempt to breed in the Nizells Avenue bushes had wisely abandoned the now unserviceable hebe bush and on 16th February I saw them adding to a nest, about one third complete, built in the last remaining serviceable clump of berberis immediately adjacent to the park's probably busiest path. Both pairs of tits obviously seemed to regard people as 'friends'. This path nest was complete well before the end of March, the feeding of nestlings began on 23rd April, and the young fledged on 9th May. Three days later I at last spotted the family in a bush in the park; two adults were in attendance and nine juveniles were perched side by side on a branch, four heads towards me and five tails! Well done the path tits! Good luck in 2008!

It now seems clear that although both pairs of tits prefer to breed in the park, if anything goes wrong they do have private gardens as their plan B. Thus if, for whatever the reasons, all their park nesting sites become unserviceable, I feel confident that these long-tailed, delightful birds will still continue to grace the gardens with their enchanting presence. But they are not the only long-tailed passerines to do so. Perhaps surprisingly, not a winter goes by without the presence of at least one visiting grey wagtail with its very long, constantly wagging tail, not to mention the winter presence of its tail-wagging pied cousins.

A Pair of Breeding Grey Wagtails, 2003

It was in the autumn of 1999 that I saw my first grey wagtail at the park's pond and since then during each autumn and winter till the spring of 2007 I have typically enjoyed up to 30 or more sightings, the earliest on 14th September and the latest on 9th March. Nearly all sightings have been of a single wagtail but on at least nine occasions two have been together and just once, on 20th September 2003, there were three together at the pond's waterfall. Unlike the situation at the seafront, at no time has there been any skirmishing. In any case, peaceful enjoyment of the pond is often difficult for the wagtails not only because of frequent human disturbance but also because of attacks by a resident robin, on one occasion aided by a chaffinch. Never once has the visitor attempted to stand its ground but always immediately flown off. Sometimes a grey wagtail would feed on the park's bowling green and when on one occasion it joined a pied the two fed amicably together for some ten minutes before one flew off.

While a grey wagtail is always a pleasure to watch, there were several times when it was most enjoyable. Once after a good dip, the bathing wagtail faced me, raised its tail to a vertical position and then for several seconds shook it rapidly from side to side forming a continuous fan. The effect was quite stunning. It is also a delight to watch a wagtail walking on the pond's water-lily leaves, thereby picking off insects and catching flies on or just above these leaves. On one occasion, the wagtail was joined on the same leaf by a female blackcap which simply bent over the side of the leaf to have a drink. On another occasion, a chiffchaff seemed to think the wagtail was walking on water and did not land on the leaf to join the wagtail but alongside and promptly sank! Thereafter the chiffchaff fed on the flies by hovering over the water and leaves but eventually it got the idea and settled on the leaves to feed in the company of the unconcerned wagtail.

The presence of a breeding pair in the summer of 2003 was a real surprise and perhaps constitutes a unique record for Brighton and Hove. Unfortunately, I had not been visiting the park much that year but on walking along Furze Hill at lunchtime on 28th June I was amazed to see in the distance a grey wagtail on a garden wall which quickly flew on to the roof of the nearby Furze Croft complex and then away. What on earth was a grey wagtail doing in the middle of Brighton and Hove in the middle of the summer? Was it just passing through? I doubted it. In that case, it must be breeding! I could hardly believe it. I returned in the early evening, this time with binoculars, determined to scour the entire neighbourhood and, of course, to keep checking the park's pond and waterfall. I never even reached the park. To my amazement and pleasure I immediately saw on the large front lawn of Wick Hall a glorious male wagtail busily feeding a juvenile already perhaps a week or so fledged. I watched unbelieving and entranced for a long time. But where were the male's partner and other youngsters? Had the local cats been busy? That evening I phoned the exciting news to Peter Whitcomb.

Next morning I found the male and youngster as before, although after a time the youngster flew into a nearby tree where the adult continued to feed it. But where was the female? After a fruitless search round about and a look at the waterfall, I returned to the Wick Hall lawn where I found the juvenile feeding by itself. Suddenly, to my great pleasure, an adult landed by its side: the missing female! Now it was the turn of the male to be stubbornly absent. Relationship breakdown? After another fruitless search I returned to the lawn to find the female now looking after two youngsters! I really was very happy. Next day I phoned an RSPB member living near me, Michael Crane, who also found it difficult to believe his eyes when confronted with an adult female grey wagtail and two juveniles.

During the next seven days I encountered only the female with a single youngster in tow. Chris Perry accompanied me on one visit and eventually we managed to locate the female on the back lawn of Furze Croft from where she was feeding her offspring ensconced in adjacent trees. One morning was most instructive and amusing. Knowing that the pond's waterfall just had to be irresistible to the wagtails, I decided to sit nearby and wait…and wait. Sure enough, the female and youngster eventually appeared. Immediately the adult flew to a stone in the waterfall, washed thoroughly, then flew to nearby railings and enjoyed a good preen. The youngster then flew to the very same stone in the waterfall, washed itself just as the female had done, then flew to exactly the same spot on the railings where its mother had preened herself and dutifully did the same. What influence mums do have on their offspring! I hoped wherever the father was, he was setting a similarly good example to his charge!

Two days later, the female and youngster had also disappeared. The gardener of the Wick Hall private garden told me he had first seen the 'birds with long tails' at the end of April, so it seems clear that in 2003 a pair of grey wagtails successfully bred in the heart of Brighton and Hove City. I wondered what would happen next in and around this little gem of an urban park. On three consecutive days, 23rd to 25th August, I saw a grey wagtail at the waterfall and since these were such early dates I thought the bird was probably one of the youngsters or breeding adults making a surprise return visit rather than the first appearance of a wintering wagtail. Needless to say, I had high hopes that the wagtails would try to breed again in future years but, sadly, my hopes have not yet been realised. But I keep waiting and watching!

The first four days of March 2007 were indeed extremely exciting, since on three of the days a pair of grey wagtails came at dusk to the pond's waterfall to bathe and then to preen. One wagtail was beginning to develop a black bib, therefore it was a male; the other was not, therefore a female. Would they remain to breed? Sadly, the female's last visit was on 4th March but the male stayed on for another five days, roosting each night in one of the pond's clumps of bamboo. Then he too disappeared, after a rather close encounter with a brown rat! Perhaps next year....

A Pair of Great Spotted Woodpeckers
Colonise the Gardens, 2005-2007

2005: The first year

Over the previous four years I had enjoyed odd sightings of both male and female great spotted woodpeckers in apparent passage through the park but towards the end of January a pair announced their residency with a fanfare of drumming which had most users of the park scanning the treetops for a good view of the new noisy residents. However, at no time had I seen the male and female woodpeckers together. Were they really a pair with breeding intentions? My uncertainty ended when on 6th February a keen photographer of wildlife, Chris How, showed me a digital photo he had taken that morning of two woodpeckers close together in a tall elm by the park's pond. Yes, they really were a pair! I was surprised because I didn't regard the park as a suitable habitat for these woodpeckers, having a hunch that there was probably insufficient food or dead wood for successful breeding. Nevertheless, the woodpeckers clearly thought differently and in the middle of February I saw for myself the male and female together, first the male drumming and then the female responding. But where would the woodpeckers attempt to excavate? At the end of February I noticed a hole an inch or so deep in the trunk of a plane tree but since the wood of this trunk was in no way rotten the excavation was quickly abandoned – much too like hard work!

Not long after, on 3rd March, I noticed the beginning of another excavation but in probably the worst possible site in the park! The hole was about 20 feet high in a partially rotten stump of a sycamore directly above the exit gate of the pond enclosure used by countless people each year once spring is underway. Moreover, the three-feet-long stump was at an angle of some 45 degrees to the vertical and the hole was not directly above the ground but some 30 degrees further round the stump. An excavation would surely prove architecturally very tricky. I could scarcely believe my eyes. This excavation, too, I thought, would quickly be abandoned, especially when the woodpeckers realised the degree of human disturbance they would increasingly encounter. Next day I saw the male peering into the hole with the female nearby but no further excavation was attempted. Indeed, in the days which followed I saw no excavation at all and assumed that the woodpeckers were trying elsewhere but, if so, the new site eluded me.

To my great surprise, when I arrived at the pond on the morning of 23rd March I saw the female woodpecker vigorously excavating at what was an obviously very problematic nest hole. For some 15 minutes she was hard at work, then when she rested by the side of the hole the male immediately arrived and began to excavate watched by the female, after which she flew off and the male continued until disturbed by people whereupon he too flew off. Surely the woodpeckers wouldn't continue at this most unsuitable site?

No surprise, then, the following morning when there was no sign of them but in the afternoon the male turned up just to stare into the hole until he was again disturbed by people and flew off. Next morning the male was once again stationary at the nest hole and later the female spent about 15 minutes absolutely motionless, just staring into the hole! Next day I saw the male once more just staring into the hole and I wondered what on earth was going on. However, on 27th March I was relieved to see that at least the female had seemingly made up her mind and was strenuously excavating, as she was again the following morning. Thereafter both male and female took turns to excavate without appearing to be in any great hurry and I was therefore very pleased when, ten days later, I saw a woodpecker looking out from inside the hole. Real progress! In the afternoon of 8th April there was a welcome further development when I saw the male not only vigorously throwing out shavings from the hole but when he left the hole as if at a prearranged time, the female arrived and I witnessed my first mating between the pair, lasting some 20 seconds, and then the female entered the hole and in turn vigorously excavated.

By this time the woodpeckers could have been in no doubt as to the degree of human disturbance they could expect right under their nest hole but, happily, they had decided to stick it out. Indeed, much to my relief, they were to become almost brazen owners of the entire pond conservation area.

Seemingly wholeheartedly enjoying their celebrity status, the woodpeckers now continually excavated on a daily basis, occasionally interrupted by a mating, but on 20th April excavation finally ceased. This meant that the excavation had taken the woodpeckers at least 49 days which, surprisingly, is a time five days longer than the longest recorded in *Birds of the Western Palaearctic* and more than double the

Plate 11   The mistle thrushes' nest tree on the East Slope.

Plate 12   The pond, covered in duckweed, showing the waterfall and surrounding vegetation.

Plate 13   Does the park look empty of birds today? Don't worry, this cheeky little bird will soon make an appearance!

Plate 14   A handsome jay on the roof of the Garden Café.

Plate 15   A great spotted woodpecker looking out from its pond sycamore nest hole.

Plate 16   A pensive female woodpecker outside the nest hole.

Plate 17   Just a bit more excavation is necessary!

Plate 18   The male woodpecker brings food to its male chick. Summer has clearly come.

Plate 19   And now the chick has only to open its bill!

time of up to three weeks Gerard Gorman had recorded in his *Woodpeckers of Europe*. Moreover, it had even taken the woodpeckers 29 days after determined excavation had commenced on 23rd March. Two probable reasons spring to mind, the first being the amount of human disturbance suffered by the woodpeckers and the second the architectural complexities of excavating in a stump inclined at 45 degrees to the vertical. Whatever the reasons by the end of 20th April the cavity was ready for its first egg.

Both partners seemed to share incubation equally and, after the eggs hatched on 6th May, feeding duties as well. Four days after hatching the nestlings were often left on their own as both parents foraged for food. If people were passing through the pond's exit gate as a parent arrived with food, it would simply wait until the coast was clear and then quickly enter the hole. On average, I noticed, the nestlings were being fed every five minutes or so. By 21st May the nestlings – though it seemed to me there was only one – were very noisy; that day I saw a head poke out of the nest hole and from then on the parents no longer entered the hole to feed their young. A few days later it was sadly obvious that there was indeed only one surviving youngster but at least this sole survivor certainly made up for its lack of siblings by loud incessant calling.

Curiously, on the morning of 28th May, I noted during a two-hour period 17 visits by a woodpecker to feed its youngster but in the 16 visits in which I had sexed the feeder I saw it was only the male on duty. What had happened to the female? I was perplexed. However, when I returned in the afternoon the very first parent I saw feeding the youngster was the female, followed by two visits by the male. Unfortunately, there were so many people milling around the pond that I decided to leave but the fearless, now quite brazen woodpeckers stayed on. Clearly it was high time for the youngster to fledge and when I returned in the evening I saw that the female obviously agreed with me. In two successive visits to her youngster she tantalizingly showed a bill-full of food but kept it just out of the youngster's reach. On her third visit the exasperated youngster caught hold of its mother's white breast feathers and tried to hold on. To no avail. I therefore fully expected such a frustrated and hungry juvenile to have fledged by my return early the following morning.

However, to my surprise the youngster was still in the nest hole looking out expectantly as always but was not fed during the ten minutes I watched. I then watched for half an hour at midday and saw the youngster fed only once, this time by the male. During another half hour's watch in mid-afternoon the youngster was not fed even once and indeed it seemed to have become resigned to starvation rations since it was no longer calling and often was not even visible at the nest hole. Visitors to my home prevented me from returning in the evening but the following morning, 30th May, all was quiet at 9am and as I watched and waited, and then watched and waited some more, all remained quiet. The youngster had fledged! Strangely, all remained quiet during the next few days and I assumed that the three woodpeckers had left the park. But on 4th June I heard by the pond those characteristic 'tchick' calls and eventually, through quite dense foliage, I spotted the juvenile with its lovely rose vent and bright red crown creeping up a trunk and expertly looking into crevices. Surely it was not already self-sufficient? Whether so or not, on the following two days I saw the female feeding her offspring both times in the vicinity of the pond. My last sightings that summer, just two days later, were of the juvenile by the pond and in the evening of the female preening high in an elm, again by the pond. Perhaps all three woodpeckers remained in the park but, if so, I no longer heard their calls.

I was mystified as to why only one youngster had been raised. Had there been too much human disturbance or had the adults not found enough suitable food? I thought the latter. But what of the woodpeckers' rather feared predatory tendencies? I saw only one attempted predation: by the female at a blue tits' nest hole which occurred on 7th April when both woodpeckers were busy excavating their own nest hole. The predation had a most remarkable outcome. Both tits defended their tree-hole nest valiantly but after failing to deter the predator by mobbing, they simultaneously landed high on its back and clung on. With both tits attached, the woodpecker dropped like a stone to soft ground some 20 feet below with the resulting impact detaching the two tits. None the worse for wear, the woodpecker briefly returned to the tits' nest hole before flying off. If, I thought, predation notwithstanding, there really wasn't sufficient food available in the park to raise a large family, perhaps the pair of woodpeckers would consequently desert their new location. I hoped not, despite the woodpeckers' unwelcome predatory tendencies. I kept a lookout and, more importantly, my ears open.

Long before this, many visitors to the park were continually informing me of their various bird sightings but I was particularly pleased to be told at the end of July that a great spotted woodpecker had recently been seen in a garden along Nizells Avenue. So the woodpeckers were still around. In the middle of August I heard once again those characteristic calls and two days later I managed to see both male and female in a large sycamore by the stream. The pair had very definitely not deserted the park. After that I had a few sightings or 'hearings' through September, and then in early October I saw, very strangely, the female gazing into her tree-stump nest hole. Thereafter I had regular sightings of only the male until in early November when I saw once again the couple together. Things, however, really livened up for me on 17th November.

I was standing at the pond rather late in the afternoon when about ten minutes before sunset I heard the call of a great spotted woodpecker and to my surprise saw the male fly to its nest hole and enter it straightaway. I waited to see if the female would join her partner but after it was quite dark I decided that the female had already been roosting in the hole when the male entered. At that time I didn't know that the pair roosted separately. However, from then on I arrived at the pond every afternoon about half an hour before sunset and invariably heard the call or calls of the male a minute or so before I saw him enter his nest hole. Once in, he never looked out, he had really retired for the night.

Interestingly, in his *Woodpeckers of Europe* Gerard Gorman writes that male and female great spotted woodpeckers maintain separate feeding territories outside the breeding season and that a male will defend his patch against both male and female woodpeckers, even chasing away his previous partner. The male, he declares, always dominates the female in such territorial disputes. My own observations are by no means consistent with Gorman's claims and it is only at the roost hole, I was to believe, that the male unambiguously calls the shots.

It had been over a month when I had last seen the female – had she really been driven off by the territorial male? – but nine days into December, some five minutes before sunset, I heard the calls of a woodpecker and a few minutes later, to my surprise and pleasure, I saw the female fly to the nest hole and enter it. Were the couple to roost together, at least for just one night? Evidently the female was a bit anxious because she kept peering out of the hole, something I had never seen the male do. Some three minutes after sunset there were more calls, the male! He immediately flew to the hole, the female emerged and seemed to fly into him, there was a brief kerfuffle, the male entered the hole, the female flew off, called a few times a minute or two later, and then silence. Not once did the male look out of the hole. So much for my original naïve assumption that the two woodpeckers probably roosted together!

The following morning I saw the male definitely harassing the female by charging at her every time she settled on a trunk or branch and eventually she flew off in the direction of Nizells Avenue with the male in pursuit. What was the male up to? Asserting territorial rights or making future amorous intentions absolutely clear? That afternoon

I arrived at the pond at the early time of 3pm to make sure I wouldn't miss anything. Intriguingly, a full half hour before sunset I heard the calls of a woodpecker and some three minutes later, at 3.25pm, the male entered the nest hole. This was the earliest time that winter I was to see the male go to roost and I assumed he was that early in order to have proprietary rights should the female return. Perhaps, for woodpeckers too, possession is nine tenths of the law! I waited until it was almost too dark to see anything but the female did not show up.

During the next five days everything appeared to have returned to normal but one morning in mid-December I saw the female fly to the nest hole, look inside, enter it, peer out, then emerge and fly into nearby trees. Evidently she was keeping an eye on the nest hole. But to what end? In the afternoon the male arrived a quarter of an hour before sunset and within two minutes was presumably snug inside the nest hole. Three days later the apparently amicable couple were both at the pond in the morning with the male drumming at his usual pond drum post while the female visited the nest hole stump before flying off; that afternoon the male once again arrived a quarter of an hour before sunset and quickly entered the nest hole. Woodpecker life had returned to normal. While it was clear that the two were once again a couple, only the male roosted in the nest hole which the two had so arduously excavated together over 49 days or more.

On the morning of 20th December something curious happened. I entered the gardens to hear such loud, continuous knockings that I immediately thought gardeners must be hard at work close by, repairing a fence or something like that. But to my astonishment I saw it was the female woodpecker pecking furiously at the wood around the entrance hole of a blue tit nestbox, clearly trying to make the hole larger. Unfortunately for the woodpecker, the hole had been protected (from squirrels!) by a metal plate. After a few more minutes of continuous and furious pecking, the woodpecker presumably sussed out that she wasn't going to be able to enlarge the hole in this way and flew off. What had she been up to? I could only think that she wanted to make for herself a roost site in the gardens.

That same afternoon at the pond I was not entirely surprised when I saw the female arrive about a quarter of an hour before sunset, fly to the nest hole entrance, look inside a few times, then half enter and finally enter the cavity completely. About five minutes later the male arrived, called once and then, after a pause, several times, so provoking the female to look out of the hole. The male then flew to the entrance hole whereupon the female left the hole without ado and with no kerfuffle this time, flew to a tree, called a few times, and then flew off. I never saw the male look out once. He was in his hole and that was that! But where was the female roosting? I never found out. From then until the end of the year I often saw the two woodpeckers together but in the afternoons only the male entered the nest hole to roost alone during those long chilly winter nights.

2006: The second year

I was really looking forward to another year of watching these two charismatic birds which had understandably generated so much interest among the park's non-birding public. Presumably the year would be much like 2005, with the couple either using the old nest cavity though with the entrance hole now somewhat enlarged by the unwelcome attentions of squirrels or a new cavity would be excavated. And I certainly hoped that this year the couple would be able to raise more than one youngster.

Throughout January the pair were much in evidence in the half hour or so before sunset, usually feeding together in the trees surrounding the pond before the female would fly off almost always in the direction of Hove Park after which the male would enter the nest hole. Drumming commenced with a vengeance in the third week of January when I once heard and saw the male drum 21 times during just one hour! It was, of course, the drumming which most attracted the attention of the general public. Only on the penultimate day of the month did something unusual happen: some seven minutes before sunset I saw the female fly to the hole and look tentatively inside before flying off; five minutes after that a woodpecker peered out of the hole – it had to be the male! Since the male was still roosting in last year's nest hole, it seemed to me that probably the same hole would be used for breeding in the coming spring. I was wrong.

Through February, however, I had no indication that the hole would not be so used except that by the end of the month the entrance hole had become quite big, presumably gnawed around even further by squirrels and probably now big enough for one to enter. Nevertheless, through March the male continued to roost in the old nest cavity, typically arriving a full hour or more before sunset. Uninterrupted beauty sleep was not guaranteed! On one occasion the woodpecker had been quietly in his cavity for some 40 minutes when a squirrel clambered on top of the nest hole stump, so provoking the woodpecker to peer indignantly out from his refuge. A few days later a squirrel once again inconsiderately clambered around the nest stump and once more the woodpecker peered out to see what was happening. I was then certain that the woodpeckers were already excavating or would soon be excavating a new cavity, almost surely in a more tranquil location than in 2005. But where?

Five days later I discovered the new nest hole, clearly very recently excavated since the exposed wood encompassing the hole was pristine in its newness. It was perhaps as high as some 50 to 55 feet in the main trunk of a huge elm growing by the side of the pond. About two feet below it was another hole, very much an old one. This presumably meant that woodpeckers had bred previously in the park before I was a regular visitor. And they had bred, or had tried to breed, in a trunk of very solid wood, much too solid! Had this old hole been fully excavated? The woodpeckers, I thought, would have to work very hard indeed to make a satisfactory nest hole in such recalcitrant wood. Surely they would abandon it as they had their excavating in the plane tree trunk the year before. Next day I spent two and a half hours in the park but never once saw the woodpeckers at work on their new hole. Had they already abandoned it? However, when I arrived the following morning I immediately saw the male make a brief appearance at the new hole before the female arrived to work really hard at excavating for some 20 minutes, already with about one third of her body inside the cavity, after which she took a well-earned rest for a few minutes and then flew off. Two days later I saw the male once again look into the hole before the female arrived to work hard once more at excavating. Why wasn't the male helping? That day, 17th March, I left for a birdwatching holiday, now fully convinced that on my return I would find the woodpeckers, or at least the industrious female, still at work on this new nest hole.

Sure enough, on the morning of 29th I saw the female look inside the hole and scope out some chippings, all the time watched by the male. When, I wondered, would I see him doing his share, as he certainly had the year before? That evening, some 20 minutes after sunset, I saw the male, calling incessantly, arrive at the pond and immediately enter the old sycamore nest hole to roost. Two days then passed and I saw no further excavation. However, after the clocks went forward one hour, I no longer checked up on the roosting habits of the male. One thing for sure, the woodpeckers were in no hurry to complete their excavation unless, that is, the cavity was already to their satisfaction. But this would have meant a very rapid excavation in what was surely very solid wood indeed.

The first eight days of April passed with still no further signs of excavation and I wondered what the woodpeckers were up to. On the ninth day both male and female drummed a great deal and then I noticed that they seemed to be spending a lot of time in and around a large and partially rotten wych elm not far from the western end of the stream. A few days later I watched one of the woodpeckers fly into the tree but not leave it; yet scan as I did, I couldn't see the woodpecker. Was it already out of sight inside a new nest hole? Scanning every inch of the various trunks was extremely difficult given the amount of foliage in the way. Again I saw a woodpecker fly high into the tree and simply disappear: there had to be a hole! And there was! But it was clearly an old hole, like the old hole in the pond elm which itself had perhaps been abandoned in preference for the hole I had just located. Perhaps history was repeating itself. Later that day, 18th April, the woodpeckers spent quite a bit of time drumming to each other as if in celebration of something. Next day, much to my satisfaction, I located their new nest hole after seeing a woodpecker land high in the wych elm to disappear behind a trunk and not reappear. This hole was extremely difficult to see, about 40 feet high, mostly obscured by foliage, but a woodpecker's head poking out of it was very visible! Later in the day I saw the male simply looking into the hole.

In June I was able to estimate that the first egg had been laid on about 18th April which meant that excavation, if it had started on 30th March, had taken only some 19 days, thus at least 30 days fewer than the year before. But this hole had been straightforward to excavate: it was straight down all the way, not, as last year, at 45 degrees to the vertical. And no human interruption had been possible.

For the next few days there was much drumming by the male which seemed to stop once incubation had begun on about 22nd April. After that I frequently saw one of the two woodpeckers feeding in the park and occasionally I witnessed a changeover at the nest hole. Curiously, not once this spring had I seen the woodpeckers mating. However, they must have done so at least once for on 5th May I saw each parent entering the hole every two to three minutes. The eggs were fertile and had hatched!

From then on the nestlings were, of course, fed regularly. On 7th May I was told that one of the woodpeckers had predated a blue tits' nest in a large hole high in an elm and although both tits had continually dive-bombed the woodpecker it had flown off leaving nest material dangling forlornly from the nest hole. Yes, these woodpeckers are formidable predators. Next day, while watching the male arrive at his nest hole with food, I saw the female emerge to lunge aggressively at her partner who rapidly retreated behind a trunk, the female then flying off and the male re-appearing and entering the hole – a kerfuffle avoided, thanks to the forbearance of the male. By 9th May both woodpeckers were searching for food at the same time and the nestlings were, as last year, being fed approximately every five minutes. Next day the menu was to change somewhat. That afternoon I watched the male behaving exactly like a spotted flycatcher, several times sallying forth from the branches of a large oak for some 10 to 15 yards, then performing aerobatics to catch a flying insect, before returning to the branches he had just left. I really was most impressed. Perhaps this woodpecker had also watched and been inspired by the passage spotted flycatcher which, just three days earlier, I had watched catching flies around the pond in its characteristic flamboyant way! Certainly the woodpeckers are omnivorous, versatile feeders. Apart from finding and digging for food behind bark and in crevices, they can search for food by hanging upside down from twigs just like tits, they feed on lawns just like and together with starlings, they eat seeds and nuts (even once observed pinching a peanut thrown to a squirrel!), they predate eggs and nestlings, they can and do visit bird tables, and they can even catch flying insects like spotted flycatchers. They are truly impressive birds. But, given this versatility, why did the woodpeckers raise only one youngster last year? I had high hopes for at least two or more this spring.

By 20th May juvenile calls from the hole were very audible but again it seemed only one chick was calling. Five days later a youngster was poking its head out of the nest hole and it became quickly clear that the adults had once again raised only one chick. What was wrong? Curiously, on 27th I noticed the female completely entering the nest hole several times and coming out backwards, surely not a procedure recommended for best feather care. When would the youngster fledge? I was anxious not to miss the maiden flight this year. During the morning of 29th I noticed that the youngster was fed only infrequently while in one and a half hours' watching during the afternoon and early evening I saw no feeding at all. Clearly the youngster would fledge the following day. It didn't! To my surprise the male continued to feed his offspring, though throughout the day I saw no sign of the female. Just like last year, the female was no longer on constant feeding duty, if duty it continued to be. Why didn't the youngster fledge? In the evening it was no longer begging for food but uttering incessant adult calls while looking out from the nest hole all the time. To my further surprise I saw the male feed it eight times at two or so minute intervals, the last time entering the nest hole and then peering out occasionally. The youngster was now absolutely quiet. Obviously fledging would be on the morrow.

But the woodpeckers continued to surprise me. I arrived in the morning at 10am and was very surprised to see the juvenile looking out from the nest hole and calling incessantly. I hadn't, after all, missed the maiden flight. Eventually, at about 11.30am, the male arrived with food but to my further surprise didn't try to tempt out his offspring but fed it immediately and flew off. Clearly, I thought, fledging wasn't imminent, so I left. When I returned three hours later I was greeted with drumming from the direction of the pond and no calls at all from the nest hole: the youngster had fledged! Once again I had missed it! More seemingly triumphant drumming came from the direction of the pond trees but the drummer remained irritatingly well hidden behind dense foliage. Before leaving, I checked the hole for a last time 'just to make sure' and watched a squirrel giving it a thorough going-over! On returning in the evening I saw the male twice in the pond elm trees before it flew in the direction of Hove Park but there was no sign of junior.

However, the following day, 1st June, I spotted junior and the male together in the pond elms and a day later I saw the juvenile accompanied by both parents, the female not only having turned up but once again carrying out parental duties. Unlike the year before I continued to see the three woodpeckers in the park. Two weeks after fledging I watched junior being fed by its mother half a dozen times in just a few minutes and I was surprised at the way it just waited to be fed. Indeed, I had never once seen this youngster searching for food on its own. Moreover, feeding by the adults continued till at least 22nd June when I saw junior being fed by the male with the female watching nearby. After that, till the end of the month I regularly heard woodpeckers calling and whenever I managed to spot one it was always junior. Evidently it was surviving.

Woodpeckers continued to frequent the park through July but were exceedingly scarce through August and thereafter made sporadic appearances until the end of October. Interestingly, in the middle of September I saw a squirrel looking out of the woodpeckers' wych elm nest hole, now considerably enlarged by its attentions, and at the end of the month green leaves and a stick were protruding from the hole. I doubted that this nest hole would be used as a winter roost by either of the two woodpeckers: a squirrel had clearly taken it over. There can be little doubt that St Ann's Well Gardens must have, unfortunately, one of the highest densities of grey squirrels anywhere in the universe!

At the end of October I noticed the female woodpecker on the trunk of the pond elm with the two holes, first of all peering into the old hole, then for two minutes into the abandoned hole before flying off. What strange behaviour. A week later I saw the male look into the abandoned hole. How strange. Both of them were now often about the park and I wondered where they were roosting. Towards the end of November, at approximately 4pm, I saw the male enter the wych elm old nest hole, still obviously serviceable, while five minutes later the female flew off in the direction of

Hove Park. However, the very next day at about the same time I saw the female fly to this old nest hole and was just about to enter it when the male arrived alongside, so provoking a brief kerfuffle after which the male entered the hole with the ousted female continuing to feed for a while before flying off. Everything, therefore, was just like the winter before, so it seemed, except that the sycamore nest hole, no longer serviceable, had been exchanged for the wych elm old nest hole. And the male continued to call the shots. But the couple were definitely sharing the park for feeding.

December, however, was to produce two real surprises. The first was that the female took over the male's wych elm roost hole! On 10th December I saw the male fly in to roost at 3.35 and then on 15th I saw the female fly to the hole at 3.15, look in for about half a minute, and then enter. I waited till after 4pm for the male to arrive and oust her but there was no sign of him! I was surprised and wondered if he had come to harm but the following morning both of them were feeding amicably together. What would happen next? In the following afternoons I saw only the female feeding before going to roost, with the male conspicuous by his absence. The second surprise was the sudden presence of an intruder! During the morning of 23rd December I saw a male harassing a female and then one pursued the other six or seven times round the bird reserve in wide circles, one of them uttering a continual staccato, machine-gun-like kakakakakaka…. I wondered what on earth was happening and then suddenly, while the pursuit was in full cry, I heard drumming! There were therefore three woodpeckers in the park and presumably the intruder – the interloper - was being made to feel thoroughly unwelcome, much to the approval of several of the lady dog walkers! Indeed, that afternoon (by popular vote!) it was decided that the intruder and not one of the original couple had got the message and had left the park. If so, it nevertheless still took a few days for the couple's agitated behaviour to return to pre-intruder normality. For example, on Christmas Day afternoon the female entered the roost hole at 3.25 without ado but directly afterwards loud calls and drumming from the adjacent large oak obviously induced her to emerge from her roost to join the oak tree's mysterious drummer – presumably her male partner though I hadn't been able to sex the drummer – and both then flew off in the direction of the pond elms. Fifteen minutes later the female returned alone to the oak tree, calling loudly, then flew to and entered the roost hole. But she had not retired for the night! To my great surprise, five minutes later she left the hole once more to fly to the oak tree where she stayed a few minutes before returning to her roost at about 3.50. I stayed on till 4pm but the male did not reappear and nothing further happened. On that Christmas Day afternoon I decided that 2007 was going to be the most interesting year yet for the St Ann's Well great spotted woodpeckers! And, indeed, so it was.

2007: The third year

In many ways the year started off as the year before with the two woodpeckers obviously a couple, feeding together, drumming to each other, and sometimes chasing each other round the park in courtship. Whenever I managed to sex the woodpecker entering the wych elm roost hole in the late afternoon, it was always the female. Interestingly, she often entered the roost hole also during the mornings, although only for a stay of a few minutes. For what reason or reasons? Once in mid-morning I saw the male fly to the roost hole and look inside but he was immediately displaced by the female who then entered the hole for some five minutes, though constantly peering out, presumably to check on the whereabouts of her ousted partner who had flown to the adjacent large oak but who then flew off when the female eventually attempted to join him. Male pique? Just two days after that, in the middle of January at roost time, I saw a woodpecker by the roost hole suddenly leave it and, calling loudly and excitedly kakaka…,fly straight towards a blackbird in one of the pond elms some 50 yards away and attack it! Extraordinary! What could the blackbird have done or had been doing to warrant such aggression? The only other interaction I saw that winter between a woodpecker and another species was when a magpie drove off the drumming male from the much-favoured stream drumming post.

In the previous year both woodpeckers had several times examined the pond elm woodpecker-excavated hole before they had set out to excavate a new hole about two feet above it. Why did they then abandon this new hole in favour of excavating the nest cavity they were to use in the wych elm? I never found out. Then, throughout January and February in 2007, the woodpeckers repeatedly examined and peered into their 2006 abandoned hole without ever trying to enter it. What strange behaviour. Why such preoccupation with their abandoned hole? On 11th March, not much to my surprise, I saw that the female was excavating yet another hole in this pond elm, about two feet above their abandoned hole, and displaced a foot or so around the trunk. Already she could get about one third of her body in the cavity, so clearly the woodpeckers had already been excavating for some days.

The Pond Elm

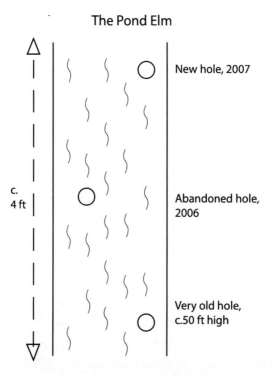

c. 4 ft

New hole, 2007

Abandoned hole, 2006

Very old hole, c.50 ft high

As in the year before, the female seemed to be doing most of the excavating, sighted hard at work some 13 times to the male's meagre three stints, although, admittedly, one such stint had already lasted for over an hour when I finally left him to it. Preoccupation with the abandoned hole still existed, for on 17th March I saw the female look into it several times before she resumed excavation of the new cavity. Why still look into the abandoned cavity? On 24th I saw the cavity was being excavated from the inside: at first it appeared as if nothing at all was happening, then after about a minute's wait a face would appear at the hole and two or three times wood shavings would be tossed out. Clearly, the new cavity was all but ready for egg laying. On 25th Chris Perry and I saw the female looking into the new hole and then on 29th, after I had again seen the female peering into the hole, I heard some agitated woodpecker calls, looked up and saw a pair of blue tits taking turns to explore the woodpeckers' freshly excavated cavity. Why, I wondered, didn't the female drive the blue tits away? Not worth the bother? Were the blue tits beneath contempt? But that was the last day at which I was to see a wood-pecker at their new nest hole.

From the following day onwards the woodpeckers made themselves very scarce, although occasionally I would hear them calling and drumming or catch a brief sight of them. I felt sure that, just as the year before, the woodpeckers had for reasons known only to themselves abandoned their newly excavated hole to excavate another elsewhere. But where? Not in any of the pond trees or in the wych elm. So where? I wasn't too concerned since I knew that as soon as the wood-peckers began feeding nestlings I would discover their new nest site. As it happened, I would be told where to look!

On the morning of 15th April, after I had seen and heard the male drumming about ten times on the favoured stream post (celebrating something?), I met a Mr and Mrs

Dennis and Anne Boddy in the park who told me that the woodpeckers had been excavating a hole directly opposite their apartment in the Vineries, a block of flats located at the western end of Nizells Avenue and which I seldom walked past in my daily tour of the park. I was astonished and hurried over, guided initially by Mrs Boddy, and quickly discovered the nest hole which had a very familiar face looking out! It was some 35 feet from the ground directly facing the Vineries, excavated in a black Italian poplar next to the park's fence so that from inside the park only a side view of the hole was possible. But some of the lucky inhabitants of the Vineries had a ringside view! I returned in the afternoon and once again a very familiar face was looking out of the hole. Interestingly, I saw that another hole had been started and abandoned a little way above it, and also that a hole had been started and abandoned in the large oak next to the wych elm. The woodpeckers had had a very busy time since abandoning their hole in the pond elm.

Probably egg-laying had begun on about 15th April with once again male and female sharing the incubation, and on 4th May the pair were already feeding nestlings. On 14th Chris Perry kindly took me round the park to identify for me its many different trees and bushes and was as surprised as I had been to see the location of the new nest hole. Three days later I could hear the nestlings calling and for the first time I noticed the male voraciously feeding at one of the two Vineries peanut feeders. Next day, with the nestlings now two weeks old, I saw that the male was not only feeding himself with peanuts but his offspring as well! Indeed, on 19th, with a calling youngster's head now visible at the hole at every arrival of food, I saw that whereas the female twice arrived during a 20-minute period with hard-won natural food for her offspring, the male during this period simply flew four times to a feeder and returned each time to ever-hungry offspring with his bill chock-a-block with chunks of peanuts! This seemed to me an extremely unfair sexual division of labour!

As had happened in the previous two years, the female more or less disappeared during the days immediately prior to fledging, leaving her partner to feed their offspring by himself, with peanuts! On the afternoon of 22nd I saw him go five consecutive times to the feeders and return to the nest hole with his bill crammed full of peanut pieces to be greeted by at least two apparently ravenous youngsters. Yes, at least two! For although only one demanding head protruded from the hole for any one feed, two very differently coloured heads were appearing, one having a red patch only at the front of the otherwise black crown but the other having a glorious red crown all over. The red patch belonged to a female youngster, the total red crown to a male. There was obviously a very marked difference in head patterns between the two juvenile sexes that I'd not previously appreciated. However, it was clear that of the two youngsters, the female was by far the more active and curious and seemingly taking by far the lion's share of all incoming peanuts. But perhaps there were more than two juveniles. However, I assumed there were only two.

The really puzzling behaviour starts now! Next morning I saw only the female youngster at the hole and when the adult male arrived bearing peanuts, only she was being fed. What had happened to the male youngster of the day before? Was he still in the cavity? Was he still alive? Compared with the previous two years, there was remarkably little calling from inside the cavity. Was this because the two surviving chicks were keeping each other company? But if only one chick remained, the female, why wasn't she incessantly calling and begging for food? Perhaps she was just stuffed full of peanuts! In the afternoon I at first heard a few calls from inside the hole but during the next half hour not once did a chick call or show herself or himself at the hole entrance. I wondered if the active female chick had already fledged and the less active male had not. But if the male chick was alone and also hungry inside the cavity, why was he not calling and coming to the entrance?

Next morning on 24th May I arrived at the nest site to see an inquisitive squirrel approaching the hole, provoking a reaction from the female juvenile but not from the male, if living male there still was. After half an hour the adult male arrived, flew to one of the feeders, returned to feed the female juvenile and then left, leaving the juvenile peering out of the hole. To my surprise and pleasure and without any warning, the youngster suddenly flew out of the hole and disappeared into a tree within the Vineries garden where I couldn't see. The adult then fed the fledged juvenile, after which he three times entered the nest hole bearing peanuts but I could see no signs of life or hear any calls. What was going on? Why was he going inside the cavity? I had a walk and returned to the site to find everything very quiet. In the afternoon I saw the adult male first feeding the already fledged and calling female juvenile and then he flew to the hole and seemed to feed an occupant within but again there was no sound or sign of juvenile life. After an hour the adult male returned and without food in his bill spent several minutes at the cavity, completely entering and leaving it several times. He seemed as perplexed as I was! I assumed that the juvenile male was dead in the hole and the presence of his corpse was perplexing the adult. Had his food-guzzling sister so deprived her sibling of food that he had died of hunger? Yet he had been alive the day before, so surely he could have fledged together with his sister? But it seemed clear that big sister had killed her weaker sibling, either indirectly by hogging all the food or, more brutally, with stabs of her bill. Gorman does write that "sibling rivalry…can be brutal" and that "larger chicks will peck and kill runts…while in the confines of the nesting cavity".

The following morning I waited 45 minutes by the nest hole but there was no sound or sign of woodpeckers, juvenile or adult. I then went to the pond and was delighted to see not only that the adult female had returned to parental duties but that both she and her mate were feeding a demanding female juvenile. But there was no sign of a male sibling as far as I could see. Once again, for the third successive year, the pair of woodpeckers had succeeded in fledging only one youngster. It was very disappointing.

Next morning, 16th May, there were woodpecker calls near the stream area and again the following morning, while in the afternoon I saw the adult male foraging in the mature black Italian poplars alongside the children's playground. The morning of 28th was cold, wet and windy and I saw and heard nothing of the woodpeckers. Neither on 29th or 30th: the woodpeckers had vanished. Then came the morning of 31st.

Naturally, I now included the Vineries on my daily walk through the gardens and on passing by I heard a woodpecker calling and, to my amazement, saw a foraging male juvenile sporting a glorious red crown. Where on earth had he sprung from? I could hardly believe my eyes. To my intense annoyance I then had to leave for an unmissable dental appointment! However, as soon as it was over I was back at the Vineries to see the adult male collecting peanuts from a feeder before flying to the nest tree to feed a calling fledgling which I couldn't locate. Time for lunch. Twenty minutes after returning I saw the adult female fly to the nest hole, look in twice, and fly off. Ten minutes after that, the adult male arrived with food but I lost sight of it. After a further ten minutes I saw the adult female fly in to a nearby oak tree, feed the calling juvenile male and fly off. The juvenile then did a disappearing trick and after a half hour in which nothing more happened I did the same. That night I just couldn't work out what had happened. Where had the juvenile male sprung from? And where now was his sister? One thing for sure, she was not guilty of the dastardly act of fratricide!

Next morning, 1st June, I saw both siblings side by side in the large oak next to the wych elm. What a great sight! They looked in fine form and both were being fed by the adult female. Whereas there was only a little red on the front of the juvenile female's crown, her male sibling had the most magnificent, luxurious red crown, the best mop of red feathers I've ever seen! On the afternoon of

4th, I watched the adult male at the Vineries twice feed the juvenile male with natural food and then four times with peanuts; then in the pond elms I watched the adult female feeding her daughter. Not once had I seen the female at one of the feeders; she was clearly, quite unlike her partner, a great believer in the park's natural food for her offspring. On 9th and 10th I again saw both siblings and again I admired the truly glorious red crown of the male juvenile which contrasted strongly with what seemed to be his rather dirty pink vent! So, in the end, the pair of great spotted woodpeckers had had an excellent breeding season but which had left me, and still leaves me, extremely puzzled. Somewhere along the line I had missed out on vital observations!

I last saw the juveniles on 13th June and exactly one month later I saw the adult couple together high in a tree, the female resting upright on a bough and the male foraging almost alongside. They seemed the perfect couple! From then on I would see one or both woodpeckers periodically through August and September, so it seemed clear that, all being well, the charismatic pair of great spotted woodpeckers would breed yet once more in the coming spring, this time in the gardens' special centenary year of 2008. And, of course, I hope so much, way beyond.

A Lone Green Woodpecker

Great spotted woodpeckers are certainly charismatic birds but I think green woodpeckers are even more so! Thus I was delighted when on 14th October 2004 I heard for the first time in the park the ringing laugh, the famous yaffle, of a green woodpecker. Not only did I hear the yaffle – of course, one cannot fail to hear a yaffle! – but I managed to see the woodpecker as well. From then until 8th May 2006, with the exception of the months from June to September, I would regularly hear the woodpecker's yaffle after which the woodpecker would play a game of hide and seek with me. But how does the woodpecker know who is trying to see it through binoculars and who is not interested at all? For invariably the woodpecker will hide behind a trunk quite out of sight of the birder but in full view of uninterested park goers! So it was always a challenge to see the woodpecker and I must confess that after hearing yaffles or series of yaffles on some 70 days I managed to see the woodpecker on only 26 days! Moreover, on only five occasions was I able to sex the woodpecker accurately and it was always a male and a lone male to boot – because I had never heard two woodpeckers yaffling to each other and I had never seen two green woodpeckers at the same time. Yes, just a lone male.

Apart from that enjoyable game of hide and seek which the woodpecker habitually seemed to want to play, there was a time when I saw it playing this 'game' for real when confronted by a magpie. One day in late January 2006 I heard a yaffle and saw the green woodpecker fly on to a thinnish tree trunk in the Furze Croft garden adjacent to the park. A jay approached but flew off when a magpie arrived and immediately lunged aggressively at the woodpecker which simply retreated out of harm's way round to the far side of the trunk. The magpie then skipped round on branches to this other side while the woodpecker simply moved round the trunk to maintain its position on the other side to its pursuer. However, the magpie didn't immediately give up but continued skipping from branch to branch in pursuit of its quarry only to find there was always a very solid trunk very much in the way. After some two minutes of such frustration, the magpie finally flew off but the woodpecker remained absolutely motionless for another half minute or so before briefly resuming feeding and then itself flying off. The jay then reappeared and when it, too, flew off, its place was immediately taken by the male great spotted wood-pecker which presumably had been watching the curious happenings from afar. This was not the first time I had seen a magpie try to attack a green woodpecker and I wondered what it was trying to achieve.

Sadly, that early day in May was the last time in 2006 I was to hear or see a green woodpecker in the park although on 21st July Mr Cannan of the adjacent Park Gate complex told me that a great spotted woodpecker and three green woodpeckers, including juveniles, were coming regularly to his lawn or suet feeders and on 27th August he said he was still seeing both species of woodpecker in his garden. Clearly, then, green woodpeckers must have bred some-where in the vicinity but definitely not in the park. It was not until 25th January in 2007 that I next heard that ringing announcement of the presence of a green woodpecker and then once more in March, twice in April, and once again in each of May and June while one day at the end of July a reliable neighbour but non-birder excitedly described to me how the morning before in the gardens she had several times heard what could only have been that unmistakeable and arresting yaffle! And it certainly is arresting when you hear the repetition of that maniacal laugh close by and for your first time! So, for sure, at least one green woodpecker keeps occasionally visiting the park but for the time being that seems to be all it's doing.

Goldfinches and Goldcrests

Goldfinches are such beautiful small birds with such a charming, tinkling song that it is always a great pleasure to see and hear them and even more to have them breeding in one's local patch. Thus in the spring of 2000, when I was watching for the first time the long-tailed tits breeding in the gardens, I was very pleased to see nearby the occasional goldfinch and really very pleased indeed to see in early June two juveniles in the pond trees. So goldfinches were successfully breeding in the park. There was no reason, I thought, why they should not.

Yet over the next four springs and summers I never again saw juvenile goldfinches despite the customary presence of at least two adults during the spring, usually near to the pond. Either they were not breeding successfully or I was failing to see their offspring. Early in 2006 I added the problematic goldfinches to my very short list of birds I was keeping a very careful eye on, namely the two pairs of long-tailed tits and the pair of great spotted woodpeckers. What, if anything, was going wrong with the goldfinches?

In the days immediately preceding my holiday in the second half of March I noted with satisfaction a pair of goldfinches once again around and about the pond. Would I see them on my return? Not only did I see them but the two were perched either side of a lovely male siskin! There could hardly have been a more welcoming homecoming! But would the pair stay to breed? Two days later there were three goldfinches in the pond trees but before long one of them was chased off, presumably the interloper. Then during the first ten days of April I continued to see just two goldfinches until one day in mid-April there were yet again three of these lovely birds, one too many! From then on, however, I was to see only a pair of goldfinches (except on 27th April when a party of about 15 made a surprise, all too brief visit to the park!).

At last, on 19th April, I saw a goldfinch collecting nest material but failed to see where it flew off to. However, three days later, strategically positioning myself, I saw that the goldfinches were building two or three feet from the top of a glorious ceanothus tree, about 15 feet high, bedecked with a dazzling array of mauve flowers, and situated at the end of a 50-yard line of low trees and bushes surrounding the Scented Garden (on the pond side) and only a few yards from a main entrance to the gardens. Observation of this nest would be very tricky if I was not to give away its location. From more or less directly underneath the nest, it was certainly easy to see but from any sort of distance virtually impossible. While the site itself seemed secure and well chosen by the birds, I was to discover that the branches of this lovely tree were all too vulnerable to strong winds and simply blew about hither and thither, twisting and turning horribly. No problem, however, for the flexible branches but this spring there was to be a big problem for its precious cargo.

From a park bench directly opposite the ceanothus tree, about 20 yards away, I could just see the top of the nest through binoculars but obviously I couldn't look only at the ceanothus tree but had to pretend to be looking, one by one, at all the bushes and trees in the long line. Very irritating. On the few occasions when I went to look almost underneath the nest, I again had to walk the entire line of bushes and trees doing the same. I was determined not to draw undue attention to the lovely ceanothus tree although several people over the various weeks did walk right up to and under it simply in order to admire its array of glorious blossom. How they didn't see the nest I'll never know! But, of course, they didn't expect to see a nest and what you don't expect to see… In the end, it wasn't people who were to pose a danger to the goldfinches' nest, not even tree-climbing little boys. It was nature itself, ferocious nature.

However, at first all went well. On 26th April I saw the pair mate in the ceanothus tree and then one of them, presumably the female, sat briefly in the nest. All kinds of spring migrants were now passing through the park and I had my work cut out trying to keep an eye on everything! Three days later I watched the pair preening together in a pond tree, then feeding together in nearby sycamores, and then unceremoniously driving away that persistent inter-loper. On the last day of April I saw through a gap in the dazzling mauve blossom the colourful female on her nest, with her equally colourful partner perched directly along-side. It was a truly beautiful spring sight.

During the first two weeks of May the female was invariably on her nest and there were no alarms except when a magpie gave the ceanothus tree a good going-over. I watched in dismay and knew the magpie would discover the nest. There was no way it couldn't. Yet it didn't! These magpies, I thought gratefully, are not so smart or observant after all. I decided not to look to see if the female had been on her nest during this heart-stopping time.

On 16th May it seemed to me the goldfinches were feeding chicks but next day, and all too close to the nest tree, the park's gardeners were trying to clear away ubiquitous fallen cherry blossom by using diesel-driven blow machines. The noise was deafening. Of course, the gardeners were using industrial ear-protectors but I doubted that the goldfinches and their nestlings were so protected. The following day, the goldfinches were nowhere to be seen and I wondered if they had deserted. Surely not. Not with their eggs already hatched.

That night problems multiplied tenfold for the goldfinches. Severe winds with gusts up to 60mph swept the south coast and I feared the worst. Early next morning I saw minor tree damage everywhere in the park with fallen twigs and leaves strewn around the ground. Had the nest survived? It had. Both adults were in attendance, both appeared very agitated, but there was at least one surviving nestling. If the nest could survive last night's gale, I thought, it could survive anything. However, the following afternoon the wind picked up once again and I watched from the park bench the branches of the nest tree being blown hither and thither. One powerful gust seemed to turn the finches' nesting branch virtually upside down and inside out. There could be no way the chicks had not been tumbled out, I thought, and went to investigate. Looking up from almost underneath the nest, I saw to my amazement an adult bird spread-eagled over the nest with wings outstretched, thereby preventing the nestlings from falling out. What fantastic parents!

Two days later there were more squalls and looking from underneath I saw once again an adult spread-eagled over the nest. In the park, a tree had been blown on to another and both were being cut down. It was a sad sight. Watching later on from the park bench I could just make out an adult on the nest and when its partner arrived both left. I went to investigate. Although the nest branch was swaying and turning this way and that in the strong gusts, the nestlings somehow or other stayed in the nest. Perhaps they were wedged in. I could hardly believe it. It seemed there were at least two chicks, perhaps three, though I couldn't be sure. All I could see for sure was one yellow gape.

From then on, the weather quietened down and in the days which followed I watched both adults regularly visiting the nest. Although on 26th May I felt sure there were at least two chicks in the nest, next day it was sadly clear there was only one survivor of that inclement May weather. On 29th May the nest was empty and there was no sign of the adults or of the fledged chick either in the Scented Garden or around the pond. However, a few days later I did see an adult at the pond and then, to my great relief, I saw the fledged juvenile at the pond on four separate occasions up to 12th June. This was the last time I would see a goldfinch in the park until mid-December but at least this lone survivor appeared in excellent condition. Nevertheless, I hesitated to write all's well that ends well.

The problem had clearly been the intemperate weather combined with the fact that the goldfinches had built their nest on a relatively flimsy branch all too responsive to strong winds. I had noticed this problem with other breeding birds. Especially in the hebe bush the nests of long-tailed tits were often buffeted and occasionally damaged by powerful winds but, of course, the nestlings had never been in danger of being blown out. There was also a chaffinches' nest which had similarly suffered and I remember thinking that the nestlings must have believed they'd been born on a big dipper! Ironically, these chicks survived some fierce gales only for a predator to discover the too exposed nest and wreak far greater havoc than any of the gales. Nevertheless, it seemed to me that vulnerability to gales had been the major problem confronting the goldfinches in the spring of 2006 and perhaps why I had seen no juveniles between 2001 and 2005. Next year, I thought, would be very instructive. And so it proved.

The lone December survivor found a partner at the end of January and then in February and March I sometimes saw four goldfinches together. However, in March a pair were very definitely nest site prospecting and I watched them carefully looking over the ceanothus tree and then, on 27th March, exploring very minutely the silk tassel bush at the western end of the café complex. Words failed me, I couldn't think of a less suitable site for their nest. The bush marks a divide between two principal paths with parents and children passing by the bush twice every school day on their way to and from school, the children often unable to resist a little climb in the bush, and in the wall of the café complex hidden by the silk tassel bush an alcove provides a sheltered space where homeless people and others sometimes spend the night. To cap it all, vans delivering food to the café often stop with either their fronts or backs touching the bush. Why even bother to prospect such a site?

On 11th April I saw the goldfinches were building in the bush! About eight feet from the ground at almost the very top of the bush, the nest was quite well hidden yet built at the end of a children's much-favoured climbing branch. The only possible explanation for this choice of site was that the goldfinches regarded the constant presence of people, even children, as a protection, not a threat.

On the morning of 19th April I saw a goldfinch on her nest and then each subsequent morning, including one when the backend of a van was against the bush and its roof only some two feet below the nest. Next day I saw two small girls beginning to climb the bush but, fortunately, they were distracted in time by their parents. The goldfinches were living a charmed life. But it couldn't last. The 1st May was the last day I saw a goldfinch incubating and I wondered if the following day's desertion was anything to do with the general 'tidying' of the park in preparation for the Green Flag inspection of 4th May. Had there been too much 'tidying' around that site? I hadn't noticed anything untoward. Had a predator discovered the nest? As far as I could tell, the nest looked intact.

For three weeks I saw nothing of the goldfinches, then on 23rd May I saw a pair feeding near Nizells Avenue, and two days later a pair in the pond willow. The two adults were undoubtedly trying to breed for a second time but where? Wherever it was, they succeeded. On 9th June I saw an adult preening in the pond willow and in the nearby large oak a foraging juvenile. From the day of the desertion on 2nd May it had taken the pair less than 39 days to build a second nest, lay eggs, incubate them, feed nestlings and fledge at least one youngster. Well done the park's goldfinches! Strong winds had not been a serious problem as in 2006 but the pair's first choice of nest site had been disastrous. Their second choice obviously not.

Another small and very attractive bird, the goldcrest, has nests perhaps also very vulnerable to strong winds but until 2004 I had never come across breeding pairs in the park. Moreover, most of my sightings had been of single goldcrests, mainly in the autumn and winter. On one memorable occasion when doing the RSPB garden bird survey on 25th January 2003, even the sighting of a single goldcrest eluded me during the allotted hour and I had instead to make do with two sightings of a wintering firecrest!

Happily, the year 2004 had been a very special one for goldcrests and breeding had almost certainly occurred. At the end of May and in the first week of June I had three times seen a goldcrest bathing in the stream, twice a male and once a female, and a gardener later told me that not only had the birds bred successfully but the family party had subsequently made a scandalous amount of noise in and around the gardeners' complex. Probably the little warblers had bred in the Leyland Cypress at the entrance to the complex but since I am unable to hear the birds' high-pitched calls I was unable to track down this apparently delinquent family party. Nevertheless, I was surprised at never once seeing the two adults and their several juveniles flitting about the foliage. Presumably they must have kept very much to the tree tops.

That autumn was to be the park's best yet for both goldcrests and firecrests! While only a single goldcrest had taken residence from late September onwards, on the morning of 14th October there were at least ten of these lovely warblers flitting in and out of the foliage, accompanied somewhat aloofly by a glorious firecrest, in the afternoon by two glorious firecrests! Next day there were more than a dozen goldcrests and after that I enjoyed several flurries of goldcrests for a few more weeks. On the very last day of the month I watched a firecrest bathe in the pond after which it flew to what was all the birds' favourite preening bush, an adjacent buddleia, and preened in full view for several minutes. I watched enchanted.

The following winter and spring were bleak for goldcrest enthusiasts like me but in the autumn things improved quite a bit with frequent sightings of one to two birds till the end of the year and well beyond. Moreover, in late February I saw two birds not just together but hardly ever more than a foot or so apart. If these two were really a pair I had high hopes of them staying to breed. Then, in early March, I knew for sure they were a pair and would be staying to breed! About half an hour before sunset a gold-crest arrived at the pond and went to bathe, hidden from sight between two brick partitions rising from the water some three inches. Almost immediately another goldcrest arrived and for half a minute or so jumped from side to side and moved along the far wall displaying to the female his fantastic vivid orange, almost bright red very wide crest with just very narrow yellow edges visible. The female just had to be impressed. I certainly was. I now knew that a pair of goldcrests would be breeding in the park in the spring of 2006.

It never happened or, if it did, it completely escaped me. I saw the pair again two days later and then had sight-ings of only a single bird till the middle of the month and after that nothing until the middle of July, after which I saw one or two birds through August and September but only one from October onwards. What a disappointment. If goldcrests had bred in the park, which I doubt, they had certainly not been very obliging to me.

Nevertheless, as 2006 came to an end the goldcrest which had remained in the park put on a wonderful show. During a gloomy late December afternoon I twice watched the goldcrest bathing in the park's waterfall. When it went to preen in nearby bushes I could scarcely see it at all in the gloom, but every so often it would open its crest and a vivid orange, almost vivid red triangle of good cheer would shine periodically through the bushes' thin twigs. It was just so inspiring to watch, a flashing beacon of good cheer from a little wisp of almost nothingness. At the same time, a song thrush was singing powerfully and beautifully from somewhere above me and I could not have wished for a more inspiring end to the old year.

Throughout the first three months of 2007 I had several sightings of a single goldcrest and once in January of two foraging together, while twice in March an after-bathe preening goldcrest displayed an orange crest, therefore a male. Once again there was to be no breeding in the park, for my last sighting of a goldcrest was on 28th March. Then, on 12th June...!

While watching a magnificent male emperor dragonfly aggressively patrolling the park's pond, I suddenly saw it change direction and fly straight at a small bird flying in the opposite direction from bushes towards the waterfall. There seemed to be physical contact, or almost so. The bird reversed direction and took cover in one of the bushes whereas the emperor dragonfly continued patrolling as if nothing out of the ordinary had happened! Just another pesky intruder ousted! I focused my binoculars onto the bird and was amazed to see a goldcrest, its vivid yellow crest clearly visible. Just where had that little bird sprung from? I really was quite amazed at what I'd just seen: Britain's largest dragonfly putting to flight Europe's smallest bird! Unfortunately, I lost sight of the goldcrest amidst the bushes and then I noticed another small bird at the foot of the pond's goat willow. I had only the quickest of glimpses through binoculars before it flew off but I'm sure it was a juvenile goldcrest. There was no crest visible on its head. An adult and a juvenile! Had goldcrests bred in or near to the park without my knowledge? It was all too possible! Yet I was not to see goldcrests again in the park until the end of August.

A few days after the dragonfly's attack I phoned Phil Belden of the Sussex branch of the British Dragonfly Society (BDS) who at the end of May had given a stimulating talk on dragonflies to our local Brighton RSPB. He told me he had never seen or heard of an emperor dragonfly attacking a bird and he suggested I write about the incident to the editor of the BDS Newsletter which I did.

The Plight of Mistle Thrushes in the Park

There is one other resident bird I have recently paid special attention to and this is the mistle thrush, not only an attractive bird in itself but its declining national numbers have caused it to be singled out as an amber-listed species of medium conservation concern. Locally, for example, Brighton Wild Park traditionally supported perhaps up to 20 pairs but in recent years only a handful have bred, if that. Nevertheless, St Ann's Well Gardens usually has one pair of mistle thrushes attempting to breed either in the vicinity or even in the park itself.

When during April 2005 a pair definitely took up residence or nearby residence in the park, I was unfortunately paying too much attention to the recently arrived great spotted woodpeckers to concentrate on the mistle thrushes. However, in the middle of May I was extremely pleased to see three juvenile thrushes feeding on the slightly sloping grass lawn between the stream and the bird reserve, which I call the East Slope; a day later two of them were near the stream with one of them chasing a fledgling robin for good measure and at the end of the month I saw just one juvenile bathing at the pond. Breeding that spring had obviously been successful. Nevertheless, I was sure it hadn't happened within the park since I believed the numerous squirrels, magpies and crows, not to mention the marauding woodpeckers, made successful breeding virtually impossible. After all, the thrushes' far too exposed nests in high-up tree forks seemingly invite predation! Presumably, so I thought, the park's mistle thrushes try each year to breed in trees in nearby private gardens or along adjacent roads and use the park only for foraging.

Indeed, a few days before I first saw the three juveniles, I watched a pair of adults finish building in an elm directly opposite my first-floor flat in Brunswick Road. This nest was only some 600 yards from St Ann's Well Gardens as the crow flies, perhaps an unfortunately all too apt description of the relevant rectilinear distance! Almost certainly the mistle thrushes were the juveniles' parents attempting a second brood and according me very privileged viewing. For three consecutive mornings a thrush was on the nest but on the third afternoon, 19th May, the nest had been ransacked. I never identified the guilty party out of local cats, herring gulls, breeding magpies, visiting crows, but almost certainly not squirrels. After that, the thrushes vanished until November onwards when I had periodic sightings of a single bird in the park.

The New Year, however, began promisingly with a pair present throughout January but then I had only odd sightings of a single bird until May and June when a pair sometimes showed up. No juveniles were seen and from

July onwards again only one bird was occasionally present. Clearly, the year had not been too good for the local storm-cocks (as mistle thrushes are often popularly called).

At the start of 2007 I resolved to keep a close watch on the park's mistle thrushes, especially after 10th January when I heard a male singing powerfully and beautifully from the bare tree top of one of the pond elms. A true stormcock! And how pleased I was when the single bird was joined by a partner at the end of January. Thereafter, however, the thrushes disappeared until late in March when the pair resurfaced (after a failed breeding attempt outside the park?) and began to feed daily on the East Slope, super-ficially an ideal habitat for them with its elliptical area of grass, some 70 by 90 yards, liberally scattered with trees. In mid-April, to my dismay, the thrushes began to build in a fork some 25 feet high in one of the trees, a Siberian elm. I was dismayed because I thought the thrushes had no prospect of successfully breeding in that location, the only saving grace being that trees adjacent to the nest tree were sufficiently distant for squirrels not to be able to jump directly into it. Moreover, I saw that the mistle thrushes were not allowing even their cousins or larger birds, how-ever harmless, to alight in their nest tree, a blackbird and woodpigeon being peremptorily seen off.

On 17th and 19th April the thrushes were joined on the East Slope by a very confiding male redstart, my first for the gardens. Since I could have missed out on this stunning visitor had it not been for the thrushes, they now became emphatically my favourite breeding birds in the park! On 19th I saw them mating eight successive times, one copulation immediately following the previous with the female shivering her wings after each mating in obviously irresistible invitation for the next.

The 20th April passed quietly with a thrush on her nest (the female apparently does nearly all the incubation) and the redstart having left. Then avian drama began. On 21st I watched a magpie in full retreat with a mistle thrush in close pursuit. During the morning of 22nd, while the female was on her nest, her partner in a nearby tree was noisily attacking a pair of protesting magpies. When two more magpies arrived as reinforcements, the undeterred thrush continued his lunging, jabbing assaults, eventually seeing off all four intruders. I was impressed! In the afternoon, watched by several onlookers, both thrushes very noisily attacked and put to flight a lone magpie, after which the female returned to her nest. Could the thrushes, I wondered, succeed in fledging young against all the odds? On that glorious Sunday afternoon children and adults played and lay all over the East Slope of grass but the thrushes seemed almost to welcome human presence!

An incident next day was very spectacular. A squirrel busily inspecting the East Slope grass was suddenly chased by an Alsatian and made the big mistake of seeking refuge in the thrushes' nest tree. Pandemonium ensued. Though the incubating female stayed put, her partner relentlessly pursued and dive-bombed the hapless squirrel which jumped frantically from branch to branch as it tried but failed to evade the thrush's ferocious jabs. Adjacent trees were beyond its reach and at the foot of the tree the Alsatian patiently watched the commotion above. The frying pan or the fire? Since staying in the tree was painfully impossible, the squirrel braved a jump to the grass and somehow or other, though pursued by the Alsatian, reached safety in a small tree some 12 yards away. I'm sure had a terrier been chasing the squirrel, the rodent would not have survived. That evening I wrote in my diary, 'These mistle thrushes mean business!'

Humans became the problem next day when some young men played with a frisbee near to the nest tree. Once the frisbee hit the tree's highest branches but the thrushes seemed unconcerned. When I checked in the evening the female was on her nest, as also early next morning on 25th. Curiously, just as I was leaving, the male aggressively saw off a blackbird and song thrush, both harmlessly feeding on the grass some 25 yards from the nest tree. I'd never before seen such unwarranted aggression but did not give it a second thought. However, in the afternoon no mistle thrushes were to be seen: they had deserted their nest which, nevertheless, appeared undisturbed and certainly not ransacked. But presumably the eggs had been predated by a magpie or crow or even by one of the woodpeckers. Just how on earth, I wondered, do mistle thrushes ever succeed in fledging young? Does anyone know? For four days there was no sign of the thrushes and then both turned up on the East Slope for two days, making me think that they would, very unwisely, try to breed again in the park. Thankfully, I was wrong. I had one more sighting on 4th May and then the two stormcocks disappeared completely.

There is a gruesome epilogue to this failed breeding attempt by the mistle thrushes. In mid-May I watched a crow raiding a magpie's nest in an evergreen oak a few yards from the park. An attendant magpie made a great deal of noise but never once attacked the crow which flew on to a nearby lawn carrying a naked nestling and systematically devoured it, piece by piece, watched by the magpie which had followed the raider on to the lawn, all the while maintaining a respectful distance of some ten yards, apparently pretending to be only feeding. However, as soon as the crow had flown off, the parent magpie immediately hopped to the spot where its nestling had been dismembered and closely examined the site's sad remains, after which it, too, flew off. Clearly, the crow is the undisputed lord of St Ann's Well Gardens. Certainly at no time on the East Slope did I see a mistle thrush confront a crow and I assumed that a crow would emerge victorious from any such confrontation. But is this assumption correct? Are crows the real villains as far as mistle thrushes are concerned? Is increasing predation one principal cause of their apparent decline in our region and elsewhere? I wish I knew.

Passage Migrants and Winter Visitors

I think spring has to be my favourite season of the year but it only really begins for me when I see my first willow warblers in the park, usually during the first week of April. I consider them the first true spring migrants to arrive and I wait expectantly not just to see them but above all to hear that lovely descending cadence which is, for me, the signature tune of spring in the English countryside. When I was a small boy I was puzzled to hear the woods around my home suddenly become alive with that so distinctive song but it took me quite a time, without binoculars of course, to track down the elusive songster. It was the willow warbler according to my trusty, constant companion *The Observer's Book of British Birds* and, what is more, that rather non-descript little bird had apparently made a huge journey of thousands of miles from sub-Saharan Africa to my quiet, remote village on the Norfolk coast. Unbelievable! This identification filled me with tremendous pride and from then on I was hooked! My love of birds had begun. Probably that tiny *Observer's* pocket book, a present from a farmer's wife in memory of her deceased husband, was the most important gift I was ever to receive and remains to this day a much treasured book.

When I write 'true spring migrant', I mean a summer visitor from south of the Sahara desert. This therefore rules out the chiffchaff, so similar in appearance to the willow warbler, which winters in 'nearby' Spain and north Africa, apart, of course, from those hardy individuals which choose to winter in the south of England. These migrant chiffchaffs tend to appear about the same time as willow warblers and though I am always happy to hear their characteristic, monotonous song, it does not have for me the emotional resonance of the song of the willow warbler.

Another true migrant which arrives probably about the same time as or even earlier than the willow warbler is the blackcap (brown cap in the case of the female!). However, unlike the chiffchaff, those blackcaps which winter on the south coast leave in early spring for breeding quarters in central Europe and are replaced by blackcaps arriving after journeys of thousands of miles from south of the Sahara. The problem is how to distinguish between late central European leavers and early sub-Saharan arrivals? It cannot be done with certainty. For example, in the winter and spring months of 2006 I saw a male blackcap in the park on 10th, 19th and 30th January, 2nd February, 28th and 31st March, and finally on 1st and 4th April, then two males on 8th April, followed by ones and twos of males and females till 3rd May. The first willow warblers were two singing males on 7th April. The question is, which male blackcap sighted was the first of the spring arrivals? I think – but only think – the male on either 28th or 31st March! But whoever arrives first, willow warbler or blackcap, the willow warbler always marks for me the true arrival of spring and the blackcap its always welcome accompaniment.

Often associated with the blackcap and with a somewhat similar though far less beautiful song is the gentle-looking garden warbler, a true migrant which has, unlike the blackcap, no wintering population on the south coast. In the three years of 2005-7, I have seen eleven single garden warblers between 19th April and 12th May and thirteen in groups of up to four on dates in between. In small numbers, attractive whitethroats and smart lesser whitethroats also pass through the park and in the same three years, 2005-7, I have enjoyed nine sightings of the former and three of the latter, the earliest on 15th April and the latest on 12th May, both times whitethroats.

For a park in the centre of the city, it is really surprising I think, to have either reed or sedge warblers or even both turn up each year for brief spring visits. On 17th May 2004 I watched a reed warbler spend all day by the stream, bathing, preening and singing, clearly accepting a large clump of pampas grass as an adequate substitute for a small reed bed! The following year a well-marked sedge warbler spent the entire afternoon of 9th May seeking out invertebrates in abundant cow parsley. In 2006 a reed warbler showed up again, this time on 5th June around the pond, mostly confining itself to singing in the surrounding bamboo, then on 10th June an individual sang nearly all morning in the Nizells Avenue hebe bush, and finally another individual sang all day on 20th June, again in the bamboo by the pond though without once having the courtesy to show itself. But the reed warbler's song is very different from the more varied sedge warbler's (especially after I've checked with my CD to be sure!). Just to ring the changes, in 2007 a sedge warbler showed up at the pond on 24th April and three days later, amazingly, a reed and a sedge warbler kept each other company at the pond throughout the day, an excellent opportunity, therefore, to compare what passes for their songs! Late in the afternoon I saw both of them together almost side by side in the pond's bamboo but neither was singing. Finally, on 13th June a reed warbler sang in the bamboo for much of the afternoon but only allowed me two extremely brief glimpses.

Generous, however, in its visibility was the glorious male redstart which showed up on the East Slope that spring on 17th and 19th April and for good measure allowed me several hours of watching it as it perched conspicuously on low branches and then every few minutes dropped down to pick off invertebrates in the grass below. Since twice I had recently journeyed to mid-Wales at the end of May with the principal aim of getting excellent views of redstarts, the visit of this glorious thrush to St Ann's Well Gardens was a real bonus, hopefully to be repeated in future years.

Two very special favourites of mine are pied and spotted flycatchers, though only once have I seen a pied in the spring, a female on 25th April 2005 which made only the briefest of appearances unlike an early spotted which appeared on the same day as the pied but had the good grace to stay a further two days or, rather, should I say, I saw a spotted flycatcher in the park on three consecutive days! My next spring sighting that year of a spotted flycatcher was on 16th May and in 2006 I had three equally enjoyable sightings on 7th, 17th and 21st May. The spring of 2007 turned out to be exceptional because after seeing one of these charming visitors on 6th May, two of them arrived on 25th May, my first-ever spring sighting of two spotted flycatchers together, and both proceeded to hunt all afternoon from the evergreen oak close to the pond. Next day, given the lateness of the date, I was surprised to find one of them still hunting from the oak but by the following day mating urges had taken over and it was nowhere to be seen. It is, however, on their return autumnal journeys that spotted and pied flycatchers make really excellent use of the gardens.

Very regrettably, none of these spring passage migrants stay to breed and although brambles were specially planted in the new bird haven, with permission from the council, to try to encourage warblers to stay on, the brambles were inexplicably removed 'by mistake' by gardeners and so as yet no warblers have bred in the park. In 2005 I had high hopes of a pair of chiffchaffs breeding when I heard that monotonous but welcome song on 21st and 22nd May but the singer turned out to be, presumably, a lone, unpaired male. Hirundines pass overhead through April but I do not think house martins breed anywhere close to the park and swallows certainly don't. However, not long into May swifts can usually be seen hawking high overhead and a few pairs of these wonderful birds certainly do breed in cavities in nearby apartment blocks and suitable houses.

The autumnal return passage of summer visitors is well underway by August, usually beginning with willow warblers and with the chiffchaff taking over in late autumn. Blackcaps are the other typical passage warbler and only once have I seen an autumnal garden warbler, this one on 7th September 2007, emerging from a mass of dogwood by the pond to gorge for a while on the plant's berries and then briefly descending to the water-lily leaves before disappearing back into the dogwood. Just once, on 20th August 2003, a gloriously beautiful wood warbler put in a star performance, feeding for a long time high in a sycamore accompanied by a rather humble-looking willow warbler!

Welcome, of course, as is any autumnal migrant, for me the real stars of the autumn return passage are the two flycatchers, pied and spotted. In 2004 a pied turned up on 11th August in a large sycamore near to the pond and seemed very much at home, remaining in the tree all day. Since it was also in the same tree the following afternoon when I went to check, I was then confident enough to phone a fellow member of the local RSPB, Laurie Keen, and invite him to renew acquaintance with a pied flycatcher! Of course, one should never do such an outrageous thing but, sure enough, when Laurie arrived next day the flycatcher was there to greet him, still in the same tree! Where it remained the following day as well! But four days were apparently its limit for it was nowhere to be seen on the fifth day, surely already on its way back to Africa. The year 2004 was a remarkable one for pied flycatchers, for not only was 11th August my earliest ever autumnal sighting for either pied or spotted flycatchers but I saw a pied on my latest ever date of 14th October, caught up, it seems, in a fall that day of blackcaps, chiffchaffs, goldcrests and two firecrests . That year the total daily number of autumnal pied flycatchers to spotted was eight to four, exactly double.

The following autumn I was so convinced of the eventual arrival of a pied flycatcher that I dared to guarantee a sighting to a slightly sceptical John Reaney, provided, I told him, he turned up immediately after receiving my phone call! On the morning of 17th August John took just five minutes to arrive! "There it is," I said. "So it is," I heard him say! On 4th September I was pleased to see both a pied and spotted in the same stream sycamore; for some reason, the spotted was twice attacked by a male chaffinch but stood its ground, once after quite a skirmish, and it was eventually the chaffinch which left the arena. Strangely, that relatively early date proved to be my last sighting for either pied or spotted and, once again, it had been a poor year for spotted.

The year 2006, however, was an excellent one for spotted though normal for pied with eight of the latter sighted. But 15 spotted were seen, starting with a single bird on 18th August, my earliest sighting, and ending with two on 3rd October, my latest. Moreover, the spotted provided some unusual entertainment, quite apart from the customary sorties and sallies. On 8th September I saw one of three spotted flycatchers make a determined effort to catch a red admiral and I remember feeling guiltily pleased to see the butterfly escape unscathed. (Only once have I seen a spotted flycatcher pursue or suss out a falling leaf but, curiously, in mid-October I saw a red admiral do exactly the same!) Later in September I watched a spotted flycatcher make a brief attempt to catch an unidentified yellow moth but again it failed. In between these lamentable failures I spent a pleasant afternoon watching a spotted make many pounces on to grass from low perches, nearly every time having to deal with attempted muggings by a robin. Perhaps it was the same robin which later in the month tried to make life unpleasant for a pied flycatcher, otherwise contentedly installed in the pond large sycamore. It seemed clear that the flycatchers in Britain had enjoyed the marvellous summer as much as the country's human inhabitants!

It was just as well that the autumn of 2006, following that glorious summer, had given me 23 flycatchers to watch, about double the number in either of the two previous autumns, because during the autumn of 2007 after that most miserable of wettest summers I saw only four flycatchers, two pied and two spotted. The first was a pied on 16th August, every so often dropping down from the branches of the elms along Nizells Avenue to pick off delectable morsels in the grass below, and then a spotted on 1st September, which I watched for five minutes as it searched for insects high in a sycamore by the pond. Revealingly, it made no sorties. The days then went by with no more flycatchers. Were there to be no more? At last, on 25th September, I saw two flycatchers, a pied and a spotted, more or less keeping each other company. At one point, again in the same sycamore by the pond, I was watching the pied perched on an exposed branch when the spotted arrived from somewhere, flying straight towards the pied and taking its exact place on the branch, the pied disappearing into a nearby tree. I thought to myself that had I just arrived in that minute or so, had seen and identified the perched pied but had then looked away for a few seconds before looking back, I would have been astonished to see a spotted! I would probably have grabbed my mobile phone there and then to book an immediate eye test!

In trying to see these often so elusive flycatchers, I should stress that a brief glance into foliage is never sufficient unless one is very lucky, because a static flycatcher is very difficult to see amidst leaves and sometimes these birds, when at there most unobliging, can and do 'freeze' for quite long intervals. During one inactive afternoon a spotted sometimes kept irritatingly immobile for as long as ten minutes at a time. So, find a likely site and watch it closely for at least 15 minutes! Good luck! In St Ann's Well Gardens, the stream sycamore seems the most favoured tree for both pied and spotted and elsewhere a good vantage point, especially for spotted, is the middle of the lawn between the pond and the stream from where the sur-rounding bushes and trees can be continually watched.

After autumn comes the season far from my favourite but at least a few new faces add much needed cheer to the now bleak gardens. Both grey and pied wagtails regularly visit, the grey to the pond and waterfall, the pied to the bowling green, the earliest grey on 14th September, the earliest pied on 23rd. A treecreeper is a most welcome but often extremely elusive visitor. In early January 2004 I watched one apparently finding lots of edibles until a blue tit attempted a mugging. Both birds disappeared behind a thick trunk, the blue tit emerging first, the treecreeper not at all. I looked behind the trunk, everywhere in the tree, all the trees around, everywhere in the park. I never saw that treecreeper again despite a search every day throughout the winter. I would have defied Sherlock Holmes to have solved 'the baffling case of the missing 2004 treecreeper'. Next year, on 10th August, a birder posted a notice 'treecreeper seen'. From then until my last sighting on 30th January 2006, I saw that treecreeper only 21 times in 165 visits to the park. In other words, despite looking really very hard, I enjoyed a sighting only once in every eight visits! Excuses? It certainly isn't true that a treecreeper systematically flies from the top of one tree to the base of the next. Sometimes it flies only to halfway up its next tree and, moreover, it can spend much time in a tree's uppermost branches and twigs. Yes, an elusive little bird. One curious thing: while watching one day that elusive little treecreeper motionless on a tree trunk, tail flattened against it, I saw it turn its head through considerably more than 180 degrees! I was impressed!

Whilst it is possible that a few of the wintering grey wagtails in southern England visit from northern Europe, the majority of them, together with wintering pied wagtails and treecreepers, are visitors from elsewhere in Britain, the treecreepers in the park probably breeding within a range of 20 miles or so. However, the last of the regular winter visitors certainly do have to cross the North Sea, arriving in Britain from Iceland and Scandinavia towards the end of September onwards. Nevertheless, only once have I seen many redwings in the park before the year's end when I saw a party of about 15 on 30th December 2005. A single bird apparently then stayed on, showing up every so often particularly around the pond, making a last visit on 30th March. I then had only eight days to wait before the first willow warblers arrived and the bleak winter was truly over! Of course, resident birds, especially long-tailed tits, had begun breeding preparations well before then.

Resident Birds and Avian Oddities

The park does quite well for breeding birds even though it is no longer the haven it was at the turn of the millennium. Nevertheless, adding welcome variety to the breeding species already discussed are collared doves, woodpigeons, magpies, carrion crows, wrens, dunnocks, robins, blackbirds, song thrushes, blue tits, great tits, chaffinches and greenfinches with herring gulls, jays, starlings and house sparrows breeding, or attempting to breed, in the vicinity. While most breeding attempts are not out of the ordinary, in the spring of 2006 an amusing episode occurred with the two blue tits who were using the same nest hole attacked the previous year by the female great spotted woodpecker. Indeed, perhaps they were the very same two blue tits who had so valiantly defended their nest and its contents. Parenthetically, I should explain that during each winter I regularly feed the park's birds on an individual basis. Because they tend to know me, birds approach quite directly to ask for food, especially black-birds who can be almost aggressive in their persistence, but also song thrushes, robins and blue tits. If I forget to bring food which is usually fresh wholemeal bread or raisins, I can be followed around and made to feel very guilty! Provided birds are continuing to ask individually for food, I continue this feeding into the spring even if parents are feeding their nestlings with my offerings. Presumably a few bits of soft wholemeal bread or bits of raisins do no harm and perhaps a little good if worms and caterpillars are not in abundant supply.

During the second half of May, the two blue tits in question were particularly persistent and would take pellets of bread from my outstretched hand. Sometimes when I was walking near to their nest hole, they would even remind me of their presence by giving a dangling hand a flying prod! However, when I realised the tits were continually feeding nestlings with my bread, I became a little concerned. The nestlings surely needed something more nourishing.

Next morning I bought a large (and expensive!) packet of dried mealworms and feeling rather virtuous, returned to the park, happily contemplating the pleasure of watching appreciative parents feeding their young with nourishing mealworms. To my surprise, both blue tits looked in consternation at the ten or so mealworms on the palm of my hand and resolutely refused to have anything to do with them! Thinking they were too dry, I went home to soak a number of them and then returned to the park, fortified, just in case, with some fresh wholemeal bread. Once again the tits refused the mealworms. I then put on the palm of my hand one soaked mealworm and one small lump of bread. A tit arrived, had a look, picked up the mealworm, tossed it out of my hand on to the ground and then flew off with the pellet of bread. That was telling me!

I don't know if the nestlings successfully fledged. One day the tits no longer greeted me and I hoped parents and fledglings were feeding somewhere high in the tree tops. However, I know I never once saw this family because I would have recognised the parents whom I had justifiably called Scraggy and Very Scraggy! Seeking a birder with a garden, I gave the packet of mealworms to John Reaney who told me they were much appreciated by visiting blackbirds, starlings and sparrows!

Only one raptor, a sparrowhawk, frequently visits the park and has been seen taking a starling on the bowling green and several collared doves, apparently its favourite diet. A kestrel is seen flying overhead only very infrequently and it is also surprising that one of the Sussex Heights peregrines is not seen more frequently. The greatest commotion I've ever witnessed in the park, certainly on the part of herring gulls near and apparently afar was caused in the middle of a summer month not by the presence of a raptor but by a visiting heron which briefly alighted in a treetop and then took off. Presence obviously most unwelcome!

The first avian 'oddity' I recall is of three woodcocks taking refuge in St Ann's Well Gardens during the very cold snap of 7th to 14th February 1991. Most of the time, however, they spent probing soil underneath trees in the Furze Croft private garden and visited the park only towards dusk when human visitors were thin on the ground. It was certainly a big surprise to see them there.

I myself have never seen a cuckoo passing through the park but I was very reliably informed that one had made a brief visit early in the morning of about 20th April 2001. I've also never seen a kingfisher in the park but several people told me that twice a kingfisher came to the pond to fish in the late summer and early autumn of 2005. On one occasion this shy bird was apparently watched fishing by several people at a distance of only ten yards or so. Amazing! Either it was too hungry to be shy or the sight of so many fish had quite mesmerised it! Why wasn't I there?! Jackdaws in the park are extremely scarce and I have never seen any making a visit. However, a reliable observer told me that two dropped by during an open air showing of an Oscar Wilde play in the park's Scented Garden but left after only a few minutes. Apparently Oscar Wilde was not to their taste.

A surprising visitor I did manage to see was a male pheasant which stayed from 19th October to 6th November 2004. Quite at home it seemed too, easily evading canine attempts at capture and also the initial attempts of gardeners who felt it would be safer if moved to a more usual habitat. Everyone felt quite sad when it finally took off, last seen flying north over the houses along Nizells Avenue. The following year I again saw a male pheasant, this time somewhat earlier on 2nd September, but this pheasant had signed up for only a day visit.

One more 'oddity' is that of a party of siskins in 2006 which took up residence in the park and its environs from at least 13th March when I first saw two females, one bathing in the pond, to my last sighting of two on 4th April. In between, there were as many as eight at the pond, with at least two marvellous males, and on one memorable day I saw two goldfinches on a twig with a male siskin in between, a truly lovely sight. When on 29th March I saw one of the male siskins offer food to a female, with gift accepted, I knew that the siskins would soon be gone, as indeed they were. But, who knows, perhaps siskins will return for future visits, however briefly, and then I'll no longer have to regard them as an 'oddity'. Who would not welcome an annual visit of a party of siskins!

Coinciding with my last sighting of siskins in the spring of 2006 was the unexpected arrival on the bowling green of a confiding and very charming white wagtail, so very closely related, of course, to our own pied wagtail. This little bird really took to the bowling green where it stayed from 4th to 12th April and then disappeared for good. Not too much of an oddity, perhaps, but my only sighting of a white wagtail in Brighton and Hove City or, for that matter, in the UK!

Butterflies and Dragonflies

In the summer months of July and August, when birds can be a bit thin on the ground, butterflies and dragonflies come into their colourful own and help keep birdwatchers fully occupied. Of course, these two very different kinds of flying jewels are not confined solely to the summer months. At least two of the park's stalwart butterflies, the holly blue and speckled wood, compete with willow warblers to be the heralds of spring, after which they appear all through spring and summer well into autumn, even October. Lending able but less glamorous support are the two well-known if not greatly loved whites, the small and large.

Of the five colourful nymphalids one might expect to see, the glamorous red admiral is nearly always first to appear, usually arriving from the continent in early May and then maintaining a presence in small numbers until late into October, often till the middle of November. Perhaps in the future, as our winters become less and less cold, red admirals will be increasingly able to survive hibernation, so that before too long I'll be seeing hardy specimens in the early winter months well before the migrant admirals arrive. And, indeed, in January 2007 I twice saw a red admiral gracing the park. Although that other glamorous migrant from the continent, the painted lady, usually arrives well after the red admiral, it can greatly outnumber its attractive rival in bumper years as on a peak day in August 2006 when there were at least two dozen painted ladies on buddleia in and close to the park but only about half a dozen red admirals.

On the other hand, in that year my last (two) painted ladies were seen on 20th September whereas my last (two) red admirals hung on till 5th November. Strangely, I've only ever seen one early spring comma, fresh from successful hibernation. Yet invariably each July I see one or two of their bright golden, truly beautiful offspring which in turn produce the August to September ones of the darker kind which then attempt the long winter hibernation. The most commas I've ever seen were four together on and around a single buddleia bush one day in September in the bumper year of 2006.

Of the other two nymphalids one might expect to see, small tortoiseshells have completely disappeared and I saw peacocks for the first time only in 2006. Although I do remember seeing several small tortoiseshells on one warm, sunny, early April day in 1992, my last sighting of one was in July 2001. Since then nothing at all! Not even in the bumper summer of 2006! But a solitary peacock came to the rescue, seen on buddleia in late July when it was accompanied by a painted lady, red admiral and comma, then seen once in August and for the last time in early October. Surprisingly, according to the autumn 2006 issue of *Butterfly*, small tortoiseshells, peacocks and red admirals are all showing major declines in the southeast corner of England, a trend one hopes so much will be only a very temporary phenomenon.

The brimstone butterfly I've seen only once, in October 2000, but to my pleasant surprise I've seen the much rarer, spectacular, migrant clouded yellow four times: in June and September 2000 and in that bumper year of 2006 in August and the very late date of 16th October. Moreover, twice I saw in that bonanza summer of 2006 a common blue on buddleia, once accompanied by (I'm almost certain!) a small heath on the wing, and then just once at the end of August I saw that most charming of belligerent butterflies, a small copper, this one adorned with a row of blue spots on each hindwing.

At the end of July 2005 I noticed for the first time a single meadow brown on uncut grass near the wych elm of the woodpeckers' nest hole. Then on a cloudless, very warm 3rd July in that special summer of 2006 I noticed another one on uncut grass in more or less the same spot and went to investigate more closely. To my surprise, a small dark butterfly was on the wing nearby and when it briefly settled I recognised a hairstreak of some kind, quickly identified at home as a white-letter hairstreak. On grass at the base of a wych elm! There had to be a colony on that elm! When I returned to the park to check, I found gardeners cutting the grass. This was terrible timing and no hairstreaks were to be seen either on the tree or on the grass nor on the following day. But next day was also bright and warm and to my great pleasure I saw two pairs of hairstreaks spiralling over the wych elm and likewise another pair over a nearby red horse chestnut. After that, I not only regularly saw hairstreaks but one morning one briefly settled by my feet at the pond, a 'long way' from the wych elm and red horse chestnut. There therefore had to be another colony in the tall pond elms but, if so, I never found more evidence of it. At last, in mid-July I had my first prolonged sighting of a white-letter hairstreak when one spent about five minutes on grass by the wych elm, sometimes right at my feet! Next day another hairstreak was at my feet when a blackbird came bounding towards me, no doubt with a bit of bread in mind, but on seeing the hairstreak made a sudden lunge at it, only to see it, to my relief, fly safely off. Two days later on a hot, cloudless 27th July, hairstreaks were visible for the last intriguing time. It had indeed been an intriguing, exciting fortnight. Next summer, I resolved to myself, I would carefully check out all the park's elms!

But there was no need. The miserable summer of 2007, apparently the wettest nationally since records began, ensured that butterflies in the park generally fared very badly. For example, throughout the entire so-called summer I saw only two painted ladies while white-letter hairstreaks were visible for only the three days of 7th to 9th July and then never more than three hairstreaks at any one time.

Coming to day-flying moths, I have regularly noted only the male vapourer, zigzagging its brown way hither and thither across the park during each August and September. However, the bumper year of 2006 also brought in two day-flying migrants, the silver-Y and the alluring hummingbird hawkmoth, the latter a great favourite of mine. An additional bonus of that bumper summer was the presence on buddleia of at least three specimens of the striking hoverfly, the yellow and black, broad-bodied, yellow-winged, roman-nosed volucella zonaria, an eye-catching resident and also migrant from the continent which surely deserves an English common name.

Generally spurning the spring months are the four species of damselfly which typically make their first appearance at the pond in late May and then remain to enchant onlookers throughout the summer months. But where do they come from? Because of the numerous fish in the pond, together with the general paucity of overhanging vegetation so helpful for the larvae's successful exit, the summer's damselflies surely breed less than successfully in that small pond. There is also a problem specific to my less than perfect eyesight. The most numerous damselflies seem to be the azure but, although the common blue supposedly has a preference for larger expanses of water, I am quite sure I have also identified this damsel as a co-inhabitant. Otherwise, my resulting eyestrain has been to no constructive purpose! Easy to identify, of course, are the other two damselflies which grace the pond, the blue-tailed and large red, although neither is anywhere near as numerous as the two blues combined.

The appearance of the damselflies sets the stage for the dramatic appearance of the magnificent emperor dragonfly, my earliest date being 3rd June. Then all through the summer male and female emperors arrive, though never more than one male at any one time, solely intent on fiercely patrolling his territory. However, once in the middle of a hot August I thought there were two males patrolling together and confidently identified them as such. To my embarrassment, one of the 'males' immediately began to oviposit! Unfortunately, I had forgotten that the abdomens of some mature females can undergo a colour change from female green to male blue. Indeed, quite unlike the colours of butterflies, the colours of dragonflies are emphatically not set in stone! Despite such potential embarrassments, I always wish the emperors would stay a bit longer than my latest date of 16th September (2006) when I watched a male (!) try but fail to catch an elusive large white butterfly.

Only infrequently appearing at the pond during the summer is the less than elegant and aptly named broad -bodied chaser which can be seen chasing every dragonfly in sight, including a frequent visitor to the pond from July to mid-September, the harmless-looking, attractive common darter. Only once have I seen a black-tailed skimmer at the pond when a male briefly appeared at the quite early date of 22nd May and left almost immediately, the pond clearly not to his liking. The last but one of the dragonflies to appear, generally by mid-July, is the impressive southern hawker, to be found not only in the vicinity of the pond but patrolling almost anywhere, and not averse to giving onlookers a very close once-over! Notorious as is the female for laying eggs in strange places, I was most surprised when one spurned the pond to settle instead on my jumper and proceeded to oviposit in it for a minute or two. However, when that happened on a day in early September, the flycatcher-spotting season had been well underway for almost a month and I had other things to do than stand at the pond to provide a stationary receptacle for the eggs of a female southern hawker! Generally last of the dragonflies to appear is the so-called migrant hawker and I agreeably remember in the middle of a rather miserable August to getting very close to two colourful males settled side by side on a bush quite distant from the pond.

Perhaps there is no more fitting end to this little account of the butterflies and dragonflies of St Ann's Well Gardens than to remember the day in June 2007 when a patrolling male emperor attacked and routed an obviously intrusive goldcrest! It dramatically reminded me that in watching wildlife the totally unexpected can always happen and that the hugest of surprises is perhaps never more than an eye blink away. Stay alert!

The Centenary Year of 2008 and Beyond

Having reluctantly brought my narrative to an end in the late autumn of 2007, I now look ahead to the park's centenary celebrations on 24th May 2008 (a date which will almost certainly be in the reader's past!). Quite apart from these centenary celebrations, however, I hope the preceding pages have demonstrated just how many avian residents continually show their own appreciation of the park in the best possible way by choosing to breed, or at least to try to breed, in St Ann's Well Gardens. Avian non-residents also show their appreciation either by wintering in the park each year or by choosing to stay for a day or two during their annual migration to and from Africa. This inviting little patch of wooded green only half a mile from the sea proves irresistible each year both to so many arriving spring migrants, tired or hungry or both after their gruelling flights, and also to so many departing autumn migrants wisely deciding to make a last fuelling stop before setting out over the sea on that long dangerous adventure southwards. St Ann's Well Gardens is an urban haven for birds and if the gardens' birds could but know about the centenary celebrations they would surely wish to add their own unique musical contributions.

But could just for that one day the birds have a human voice, they would also surely have very pertinent criticisms to make of many past actions of some of the council officials and gardeners responsible for looking after the gardens. They would complain of far too much of their foraging undergrowth having been cut back in winter months, of bushes having been trimmed in spring even with nests being built in them, some perhaps already containing eggs or nestlings. They would wonder why gardeners do not pay more attention to the wise provisions of the 1981 Wildlife and Countryside Act. They would wonder how it could come about that many park officials know so much about the park's flora and yet so little about its fauna. They would wonder why Green Flag judges award a maximum of only some two percent of total marks when they supposedly assess each year the council's supposed protection of the park's birds and other fauna and they would surely wonder why the city council apparently accepts without question such a startling lack of proper concern for the park's wildlife. They would surely wish to ask why, so often in their practice, council officials manage the park as if they do not know that very many British people passionately watch birds and wildlife and that over one million people are members of the Royal Society for the Protection of Birds. But these facts are certainly known by the council which has published the ecologically praiseworthy 1998 public relations document "Wildlife for People" and the, on paper, ecologically admirable 2007 "Conservation and

Management Plan for St Ann's Well Gardens". Accordingly, and above all, the park's birds would ask the city council to take whatever measures are necessary to ensure that the practice of all its park officials and gardeners is in future exactly that described and advocated by the council in these two most impressive documents. Finally, the birds would undoubtedly ask, with all requisite tact and courtesy, for the centenary date of 24th May 2008 to mark the beginning of a new era of much greater care by the council of the birds of St Ann's Well Gardens. Indeed, do not our avian friends deserve the greatest possible care?

And our friends the birds surely are. If friends are those special beings who raise our spirits when we are down and can even raise them further when we are not down, then birds are surely our friends. In those bleak late December twilights, who does not feel uplifted by the tuneful repetitions of the song thrush? Who can fail to sense that 'blessed Hope', so movingly expressed by Thomas Hardy in his poem 'The Darkling Thrush'? And in St Ann's Well Gardens there is nearly always that special winter delight of watching a grey wagtail bathing in the pond's waterfall. In spring, of course, blackbirds and robins join with the park's song thrushes in an avian chorus of joy, supported by wrens and chaffinches and, above all, by transient blackcaps and willow warblers. What would spring be like without these incredible birds and their beautiful melodies? Could Rachel Carson have thought of a more compelling title for her grim warning about the devastation the then uncontrolled use of DDT was inflicting on the planet's birdlife? *Silent Spring* was the title and anyone who has been in St Ann's

Well Gardens in springtime will shudder at the seemingly unthinkable prospect of silent springs. No less unbearable would be the absence of those colourful jewels of sunshine, the park's butterflies and dragonflies, which so ably fill the void left by those apparently absent birds during the summer months. Happily, in autumn the spring migrants return and I for one wait anxiously to be able to watch the antics of that most charming and charismatic of small birds, the spotted flycatcher, now fast declining in numbers.

There is yet another delight possible. For if we regularly feed the park's birds with peanuts, bits of wholemeal bread, raisins and such like, then they quickly recognise us and come to us to be fed if they so wish. How very special it is to have truly wild birds such as blue tits and robins coming fearlessly to one's hand to select a tasty morsel. There is indeed something heart-warming about a song thrush flying perhaps some 50 yards on recognising someone in the park and landing inches from the person's feet, looking upwards at his or her face and waiting for that raisin to appear! But, of course, these special, individual relationships are not necessary for everyone to know that birds are our friends. Without them life would be bleak, bleak indeed. In St Ann's Well Gardens people have many, many friends and long may such friendships be genuinely cherished by the city council and richly enjoyed by the city's human inhabitants.

Notes

A comprehensive field guide to British birds is by Peter Holden and Tim Cleeves, *RSPB Handbook of British Birds* (Christopher Helm, 2nd edition, 2006).

A history of the West Pier up to 1998 can be found in Fred Gray, *Walking on Water: The West Pier Story* (The Brighton West Pier Trust, 1998).

On the marvels and mysteries of bird migration, see Thomas Alerstam's beautifully written *Bird Migration* (Cambridge University Press, 1990) and also Peter Berthold's excellent *Bird Migration: A General Survey* (Oxford University Press, 2nd edition, 1999).

I've taken information on starling feeding behaviour from Christopher Feare, *The Starling* (Oxford University Press, 1984).

For information on the history of the peregrine falcon in Sussex, see Paul James, *Birds of Sussex* (Sussex Ornithological Society, 1996). The RSPB has produced a very nice informative booklet on peregrines with the title *Peregrines: Fastest Birds in the World.* For general information, see Derek Ratcliffe, *The Peregrine Falcon* (T and AD Poyser Ltd, 2nd edition, 1993).

The Regency Square Area Society gives an account each year of the Sussex Heights breeding peregrines on its website http://www.regencybrighton.com/birds/.

In her book *St Ann's Well Gardens, Hove,* Judy Middleton gives a very detailed, absorbing history of the park.

Each burst of drumming by the great spotted woodpecker consists of about a dozen or so blows with its bill in less than one second, the one oscillograph in Gerard Gorman's book showing a burst of about 0.7 seconds. See his excellent and detailed *Woodpeckers of Europe: A Study of the European Picidae* (Bruce Coleman, 2004).

"Never still", writes the *RSPB Handbook* on page 255 about the habits of the treecreeper. But at least on one occasion I have seen a treecreeper quite still, pressing itself against the bark of a trunk.

For information on the prestigious Green Flag Award Scheme, contact the Civic Trust, 5th Floor, Century Buildings, 31 North John Street, Liverpool L2 6RG or see its website http://www.greenflagaward.org.uk. I am hopeful that in future the Award Scheme will value more highly than hitherto the importance of birds and other wildlife in our parks and green spaces.

For general information on birdwatching in Sussex, see the excellent guide by Adrian Thomas and Peter Francis, *Best Birdwatching Sites in Sussex* (Buckingham Press, 2003).

Excellent field guides to British butterflies and dragonflies are Richard Lewington, *Pocket Guide to the Butterflies of Great Britain and Ireland* (British Wildlife Publishing,

2003), JA Thomas, *Guide to the Butterflies of Britain and Ireland* (Philip's, 2007) and Dan Powell, *A Guide to the Dragonflies of Great Britain* (Arlequin Press, 2001).

Useful Addresses, Telephone Numbers and Websites

Royal Society for the Protection of Birds (RSPB), The Lodge, Sandy, Bedfordshire SG19 2DL, telephone 01767 680551. The regional head office is at 42 Frederick Place, Brighton BN1 4EA, telephone 01273 775333. The website for the thriving Brighton and District local group is www.rspb.org.uk/groups/brighton. It goes without saying, though I'll say it anyway, that anyone who cares anything about birds should be a member of the RSPB.

Shoreham District Ornithological Society (SDOS) covering Shoreham, Brighton, Worthing, Steyning and Storrington, website www.sdos.org.

Sussex Ornithological Society (SOS), website www.sos.org.uk.

Sussex Wildlife Trust, Woods Mill, Shoreham Road, Henfield, West Sussex BN5 9SD, telephone 01273 492630, website www.sussexwt.org.uk.

Butterfly Conservation, Manor Yard, East Lulworth, Wareham, Dorset BH20 5QP, telephone 01929 400209, website www.butterfly-conservation.org.

British Dragonfly Society (BDS), website www.dragonflysoc.org.uk.